SUCCESS
MADE SMALL

Step-by-Step Guide to Small Business Success

BOB WEIR

Dedication

To Judy, Laura and Michael. I can't thank you enough. You are what brings the greatest meaning to my life.

A catalogue record for this book is available from the National Library of New Zealand.

Published by Under 5 Small Business Ltd

Design by Nick Turzynski, redinc. Book Design

www.under5smallbusiness.com

Contents

Introduction

It's so pleasing to see that you're looking to improve your business through reading books like this, I love to see owners of very small businesses achieve the success they seek, as well as deserve. This book is targeted at owners of very small businesses, typically those with fewer than five staff.

I've endeavoured to make this book as accessible to you as possible, covering a wide range of areas that reflect the diverse skills that you need as an owner of a small business. I recognise you don't have the same luxury of turning to your marketing expert, human resources specialist, business development and strategy manager, information technology executive, personal assistant or legal counsel that exists within big businesses. However, you need to know about every one of those areas. I've written this book with this in mind.

In developing this book, I have not only drawn from 30 years of my own experience, education and training, but I've also read numerous books, scientific papers, websites, blogs, pretty much anything I can get my hands on (yes, I enjoy reading) to inform my writing. I talked to psychologists, business brokers, bank managers, angel investors, insurance brokers, software providers, IT specialists, leadership development experts, marketing experts, social media specialists, accountants and a large range of small business owners like you from a wide range of industries. In short, I have collected all this knowledge and everything I could get my hands on to make the complex and detailed information out there available to you. You may be able to access much of this information yourself. (I've included a lot of the background information in the resource material). However, I know that, as a busy owner of a small business, you are unlikely to have the time (or desire) to look for it. That's why I've put in the effort, so you don't have to.

Less is more!

> *"I have already made this paper too long, for which I must crave pardon, not having now time to make it shorter."*
> — **Benjamin Franklin, 1750, letter to the Royal Society of London on electricity**

In writing this book, I've kept in mind this Benjamin Franklin quote. The concept of brevity in one's writing was penned many centuries ago but has been repeated not only by Franklin but by many other famous people, including Mark Twain, Woodrow Wilson, Martin Luther and Pascal. I have covered many aspects of what your small business will need. I have kept the details in each area as short as possible so you can get the most business know-how as succinctly and quickly as possible.

☞ *As a small business owner, you don't have the resources to access the wealth of material that a large corporation does. However, the concepts they use are no less important for you just because of your size. In writing this book, I have taken the best aspects and principles of big business and distilled them into concepts that are accessible for your small business.*

There is no reason why you shouldn't benefit from the concepts that the big guys get from the Harvard, Columbia, London and Stanford business schools. The success of your small business should not be seen as less important than the success of any business. However, given your busy schedule, it's necessary to present it just a little differently, so you can get to grips with it in a manageable way.

☞ *While we're talking about success, let me clarify one thing: it is not for me, or anyone else, to define what success means for your business. This is a very important theme of the book. Only you can define what success looks like for your small business.*

Questions

As you work your way through this book I will be asking you questions at the end of each chapter. This is to prompt you to ask yourself what you can do to help your small business. I am hoping reading each chapter will pose many more questions and answers so you can make your small business the success you want it to be

Complete Your Strategic Plan

As you work your way through this book you may solidify some thoughts about how you want to start your business or improve your business. If you have answers to the questions asked, and want to start putting actions in place, start writing those actions down. You can do this in a format that suits you. You can use the material on our website, www.under5smallbusiness.com or you can use the template at the back of the book.

Where can you learn more?

Subscribe to my website for a full set of templates, videos, questionnaires and additional material that you can use in conjunction with this book to deliver the specific actions your business requires. The website will guide you through the detail you need to deliver on the key themes in this book. Head here:

www.under5smallbusiness.com

Let me know via the website if I can help you in any way. Thank you once again for joining me and taking this step towards your business success. I sincerely hope this book helps you achieve it.

Chapter 1
What Does Small Business Success Mean?

What is business success and what is business failure?

Let's quickly define business success and business failure. Both concepts can raise strong emotions for business owners.

> *"Success is not final, failure is not fatal: it is the courage to continue that counts."*
> — **Winston Churchill**

The *Oxford English Dictionary* defines 'success' as:
> *The accomplishment of an aim or purpose.*

It defines 'failure', unsurprisingly and rather unimaginatively, as:
> *A lack of success.*

The line between your small business and your personal life is very blurred. Success in one will impact on the success in the other. You will often find people define business success in terms of significant growth in revenue, profit, market share or the number of employees.

The really successful business owners are often considered to be those who take their business from an idea to the top of their industry, with no money, then go on to achieve personal wealth, recognition and even fame. I will discuss some of the businesses that fit into this category of success. However, in this book, I don't define success in these terms. If you accomplish the aim and purpose that you set out to achieve, your business has been a success. It is not for me or anyone else to define that for you.

☞ *Success in your business is defined by one thing and one thing only — you!*

A small business success story

Let me share a personal small business success story from my own family:

My father was an electrician. He married my mum in 1959 and they bought a block of land for £180. A little after I was born, in 1964, Mum and Dad started JP & EA Weir Electrical Contractors. Dad wired houses, did repair work, and a lot of light commercial installations.

The core purpose for their business, while not written on a wall, was building a loving home, and feeding and educating their family. The business and home were based on an unwavering set of values centred, again, on the family. Dad always did what he said he would for every customer. He was totally honest and did a quality job. He never had a goal to grow the business.

When Dad retired in 1995, I asked him if he thought his business was a success. In his best Australian vernacular, he said, "Yeah, I reckon I'm a pretty good electrician. My trade teacher said I wasn't smart enough to get a trade but I scraped through. I wasn't much of a businessman and it wasn't much of a bloody business."

I have thought about this statement often since he said it and I've challenged Mum and Dad on it. The business lasted over 30 years. They put five kids through university. They now have a heap of grandkids and a house worth more than $2 million (on the same block of land) that they never want to leave. They have been married nearly 60 years, have a solid pension, and have never wavered from their original core purpose or values.

From my point of view, they have absolutely succeeded in achieving what they set out to achieve 50 years ago, even if they were a little modest in admitting it.

Why focus on small businesses?

If your business is really small, this book is right for you. Businesses like yours are often called 'solos' or 'non-employer businesses', sometimes 'micros', or 'Small to Medium-sized Enterprises' (SMEs).

To complicate an already confusing array of words, these terms can mean different things in different countries.

For example, in New Zealand an SME is a business with fewer than 19 staff. In the USA has fewer than 250 people. In Europe, a small business has fewer than 50 people. In Australia, it has fewer than 15.

Similarly, a 'micro business' in Australia has one to four people. In the USA, one to six. In Europe, it's one to ten people.

Throughout the book when I speak of small businesses I mean really small businesses, typically those with fewer than five staff. That is: you have five or fewer people in your business. It could be a business that is only you. However, the principles I cover in this book apply equally to slightly bigger small businesses.

In connecting with me through this book, I must assume you are thinking about how you can better run and succeed in your business. You may run a hairdresser's salon, a car repair shop, a corner store or coffee cart; you may be a painter or run a lawn-mowing business; a social media provider, web developer, copywriter or real estate agent. You could own and run one of the thousands of different types of small businesses that exist in New Zealand or around the world.

As a smal business, you may wonder at times "Who cares?" when you are but a grain of sand on the business and economic landscape.

Consider a few statistics on what some of the big guys earn each year.

- Fonterra — $17.2 billion/year
- Fletcher Building NZ — $9 billion/year
- Walmart (USA) — $380 billion/year
- BP — $290 billion/year
- Samsung — $205 billion/year
- General Electric (GE) — $177 billion/year
- Deutsche Bank — $123 billion/year

Just to give you another perspective, Walmart's earnings are larger than the Gross Domestic Product (GDP) of countries like Denmark, Singapore, and Malaysia. General Electric makes more money than New Zealand. These five companies combined (and they aren't the five biggest either) make around the same as South Korea makes in a year. (By the way, South Korea is the 15th largest economy on the planet.)

You may feel a little overwhelmed when you see these figures. And yet, we can shine a different light on the role of small businesses based on the statistics of the economies in which they operate.

- In 2010–11, in New Zealand, non-employing businesses and micro businesses accounted for 60% and 24% of total companies respectively, i.e. 84% of companies in New Zealand employ fewer than five people.
- In 2010–11, in Australia, approximately 95% of companies were in the non-employing or micro business population, which comprises businesses employing between zero and four employees.
- In 2012, in the USA, there were approximately 23 million companies that were solos (or non-employer businesses). This contributed approximately $US 1,000 billion to the United States' GDP.

- Almost 90% of these businesses earn less than $US 100,000 per year. (Walmart earns that amount of money in fewer than 10 seconds. Sorry to depress you.)
- In the United Kingdom, almost 63% of private sector businesses (around 3 million companies) were solo businesses. UK micro businesses with fewer than 10 employees accounted for 32% of private sector employment.

Most other countries show similar trends. So what is this telling us?

- Individually, we are small. Really small. However, in terms of the number of companies, there are more of us than any other sized business in the world and by a very long margin.
- We employ huge numbers of people even though each of us employs fewer than five. Most of us are alone, employing no-one.
- We contribute billions of dollars to our economies.
- We do all this and don't make a lot of money in the process.

As the owner of a small business, you are the decision-maker. You have no strategy or business development department. No R&D department. No CEO to jump on when the annual results are down. No personal assistant to book your hotel room. No marketing guru to promote your next product. No CFO to organise your funding strategy.

You need to have enough knowledge in each of these areas to make the right (or at least the best) decisions and know when you need to call on someone else's help. You do not and cannot be expected to be an expert in all or even any one of these areas.

More importantly than all these aspects of your business is *you* and your wellbeing. In a large business, if the boss strikes any personal issues or illness, the company will find a way to carry on. On the other hand, if you aren't well or fit to make good decisions, your business could be in real trouble or even disappear.

So it wouldn't be enough to discuss small business without spending a large proportion of the book talking about you, the person and the owner.

Of course, owning and running a small business can be extremely rewarding. But it can also break your heart.

What this book will do for you

My goal is to help you build a successful business, where success may mean something very different for you than it does for other business owners. If you want to remain solo or small, this book is for you. If you want to increase the size of your business from a non-employer to a small employer, I will guide you on how to do that too. The tools in this book will make you the successful small business owner you hope to be, as well as equipping you to become an exceptional larger business, if that's where you want to head.

You may be small. You may have limited capital, tight cash flows and be balancing a raft of roles. However, this does not mean you can't approach your business with the same

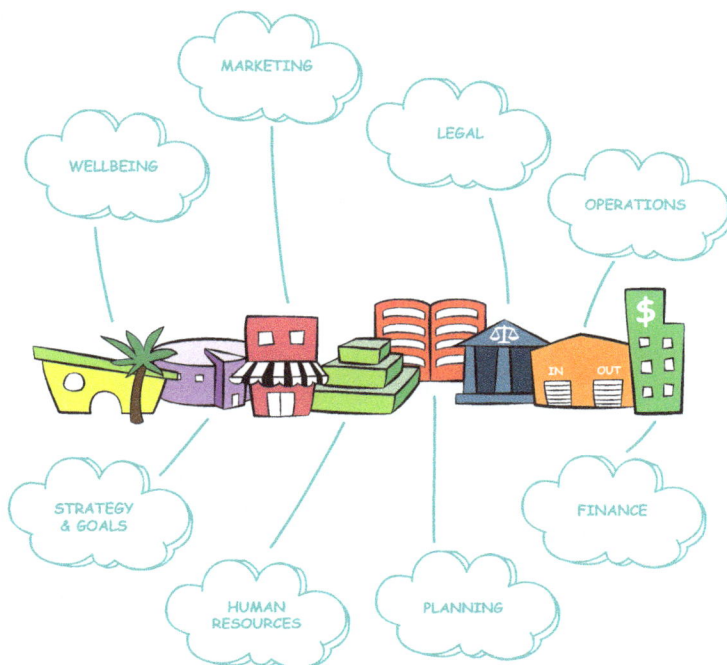

Fig. 1: The small business

professionalism, passion and tools that a larger business does.

Most importantly, I sincerely hope this book helps you to enjoy your business and allows you to reach a level of **fulfilment** and **meaning** that often eludes many in business.

What this book won't do for you

- *It won't give you all the answers.*
  Many self-help books offer you the world. This one doesn't. Business doesn't work that way. Your business may be small but you operate in a large complex world. The circumstances your business faces are not the same as those faced by equivalent businesses anywhere else in the world. You are unique. This book helps you simplify *your* world and understand the particular reality where *you* operate.
- *It won't make decisions for you.*
  As this book will highlight, you need to surround yourself with the best advice you can afford. However, advisors may think they know what's best for you. Have faith in

your own ability and don't be afraid to make your own decisions. No-one knows your business or has the passion for it like you do.

- *It won't help you control the uncontrollable.*
  Too many businesses sink into a victim mindset, blaming factors outside their business for issues they face. This is why the Serenity Prayer can be a relevant reminder when we start feeling like the victim. We will discuss how to maintain awareness of such factors. However, the focus of this book is *what you can do, not what can be done to you*.

> *God grant me the serenity to*
> *Accept the things I cannot change;*
> *Courage to change the things I can;*
> *And the wisdom to know the difference.*
> — **Alcoholics Anonymous version of Reinhold Niebuhr's** *Serenity Prayer*

- *It won't create more hours in your day.*
  While I do hope this book will allow you to get far more out of your business, it can't create a longer working day for you. If you want to bring sustainable change in your business, you need to plan and set aside time to bring about that change. Continuing to do what you have always done will only produce what you now have. If that is not good enough for you, make the time to do something about it.

Questions

- What does 'success' look like for your small business?
- What areas of your small business do you most want to focus on to achieve success?

Chapter 2
Start With You: Is Your Business Bringing You Happiness?

Nothing will contribute more to reaching success in your small business than **YOU**. The more you grow in your understanding of yourself and the more you care for your own wellbeing, the greater the likelihood of achieving the success you seek for your business. As you are the greatest contributor to your business's success, it is not by chance that this is the first area I'm covering.

Your wellbeing comes before our discussion on strategy, planning, marketing, staff or finances. You need to come first in your business's priorities.

You are the business's greatest strength. But also its greatest threat.

Too often we apportion the success or failure of our business to external factors: the economy; the government; new laws; suppliers; our competitors; unpredictable customers. It is true that many factors external to your business could lead to your business failing to achieve what you desire. However, success or failure is nearly always driven from the owner, including your ability to see these external challenges and take action to deal with them.

Therefore, a book that discusses how to run a successful small business needs to detail how you might know, manage, care for, and nurture yourself.

Your wellbeing and happiness are likely to be tightly interlinked with the state of your business. Your ability to think clearly and to make wise decisions will be dependent upon a healthy state of mind. Your physical and emotional strength will help you battle through the tough challenges that you'll inevitably face. You need to be healthy for the business to be healthy. When the business is healthy, your ability to manage stress and feel happy will be much greater.

The quality of your decisions will make or break your business. You don't have the luxury of relying on someone else to do this when you are not at your best. The quality of your decisions will decline when you are tired, stressed, unhappy, distracted and not focused on the moment at hand. Therefore, how you are going is not just a lifestyle consideration. It goes to the heart of your business.

Can running your business make you happy?

*"We hold these truths to be self-evident, that all men are created equal, that they are endowed by their Creator with certain unalienable Rights, that among these are Life, Liberty and the **pursuit of Happiness**."*
— from the Declaration of Independence, Thomas Jefferson

The pursuit of happiness would seem a lofty goal for any small business. However, if your business is not contributing to your happiness then you may question why you are doing it.

Thomas Jefferson stated that happiness is an 'unalienable right', but it is by no means guaranteed. Achieving happiness through your business (and life) is a process, a journey or a 'pursuit', not a goal or set of goals to be sought out and then ticked off as you achieve them.

So what is it to be 'happy'? How might you achieve greater happiness as the owner of a small business? And why is this an often misunderstood concept?

The *Oxford English Dictionary* defines 'happy' as:

Feeling or showing pleasure or contentment.

To me, this seems a rather superficial definition of happiness.

Russ Harris, in his book *The Happiness Trap*, has a much more appropriate definition of happiness:

To live a rich, full, and meaningful life.

Happiness is not a continual state of contentment or feeling good. That is simply an unrealistic situation. In life and business, you'll meet challenges; you will suffer inevitable hardships, self-doubt, and even grief that business can throw at you.

We are vulnerable to a fear of shame, failure, rejection or loss. Those who accept this vulnerability as a normal part of a rich and meaningful life are more likely to be happier in their business and take the risks that may be required.

Your personal life and your business will be exposed to risks. To succeed you must embrace these risks. If you are paralysed with the fear of failure and the perceived unhappiness it may bring, you will not achieve the richness that might otherwise come your way.

Your challenge is not to avoid these risks and challenges, but to accept them as a normal part of a meaningful life and build resilience to survive and then thrive when they confront you.

There is evidence that happiness is influenced by genetics. There have been many studies carried out on identical and fraternal twins. These studies showed that twins reported similar levels of happiness even when they had lived through very different life experiences. These studies indicate that no matter what the circumstances, we are born with a particular baseline that originates from our parents. Therefore, some of us will find happiness comes more naturally than it does for others.

When a joyous or pleasurable event occurs, our happiness goes up for a short period, but soon returns to this baseline. Likewise, if we are faced with a traumatic event, we will drop in happiness, but again, with time, we will return to that same baseline. There can be circumstances where a traumatic event is of such significance that when we do return from the trauma, our baseline is at a lower level of happiness than before the event. In business life, for example, this could be the liquidation of your business or personal bankruptcy.

The challenge is to build your resilience so you can reduce the number, the depth and the duration of these drops. Most importantly, if a severe event occurs, you can get back on your feet and move on in your business.

Resilience should also help you lift your happiness baseline over time. While some of us are wired genetically to be a little happier and more optimistic than others, we can all build our resilience and with it our ability to live a little happier than we otherwise would. We cover a little more on your resilience shortly.

This is only part of the story. There is a great deal more that will contribute to your happiness. In her book *The How of Happiness*, Sonja Lyubomirsky states that about 50% of our happiness baseline is determined by genetics with only 10% determined by differences in life experiences and circumstances. The remaining 40% comes from our intentional behaviours. Therefore, the key to our happiness is not necessarily in changing our circumstances, nor our genetic make-up (which is beyond our control), but in the intentional day-to-day choices we make and actions we take.

☞ *Leading a truly rich life is more about the attitudes within us than the circumstances around us. If the circumstances surrounding our business are making us miserable, changing them may help. Yet, that alone may not be enough. You may need to look to your attitude towards the business.*

We all know what the elation of a personal or business success feels like, just as we know the feeling of bitter disappointment. The danger of seeking the continual highs is that it is unsustainable and we will almost always fall back to a baseline of happiness that defines us. We don't want to find ourselves on a happiness treadmill. We need to look at our baseline — where we return after those short-lived highs or those tough lows.

How stressed are you?

What is stress?

The World Health Organization (WHO) defines stress relating to our work environment as:

> *The response we may have when presented with work demands and pressures that are not matched to our knowledge and abilities, and that challenge our ability to cope.*

Pressure in business will be unavoidable. This pressure may keep us alert, motivated, able to work and learn, and lift our performance, depending on our available resources and personal characteristics. However, if that pressure becomes excessive or otherwise unmanageable, it may lead to stress.

Prolonged and severe stress can damage our health, relationships and the performance of our business. Yet, the right amount of stress is quite stimulating. We experience this with those events that we're sometimes crazy enough to do, like bungy jumping, parachuting, or a rollercoaster ride. I'm sure you can think of similar situations in your business life that gave you this same buzz. In these cases, the stress is transient or you may frame the stress in a positive way.

Stress is a very personal thing. What stresses you may have absolutely no impact on others in the same situation. If two people are exposed to the same set of traumatic situations, the emotional and mental impact on one can be vastly different from that on the other.

We may each interpret the common signs of stress in different ways. If we are pursuing something that we love that brings us meaning, we are far more likely to be positive about how we deal with stress symptoms. However, in other circumstances, some of us look upon the stress symptoms as a serious threat to our wellbeing. In this case, the impact of the stress becomes almost self-fulfilling. It does indeed affect our health and can reduce our life expectancy, as researchers from the University of Wisconsin-Madison found in 2012. If stress becomes severe or prolonged, you should take heed. It diminishes your ability to make good business decisions too.

The major factor that determines our stress levels is not what exists in our work environment, but what happens inside us, in our thinking. To understand this, you first need to recognise the difference between pressure and stress. We talk about pressure and stress as if they are one and the same, but they're not. Pressure is the external demand in the environment. Everyone has pressure in his or her work life. That is not stress. Stress is what people do in their minds with that pressure.

Our response can be described as a state of mind or our perception of the event or circumstance. It may not reflect in any way the state of reality as it appears to everyone else.

Robert Sapolsky is a professor at Stanford University, and one of the world's leading neuroscientists and experts in stress. In studying wild baboon populations in Kenya, Sapolsky examined how prolonged stress can cause physical and mental afflictions in some animals and, more importantly, in humans.

Sapolsky described what is physically happening when animals, including humans, are stressed. There is a release of hormones (adrenalin and glucocorticoids). These hormones can have a range of impacts on us. In the wild when an animal is faced with real stress (i.e. being eaten), its attention is focused entirely on survival. In his book *Why Zebras Don't Get Ulcers*, Sapolsky discussed his view that animals such as zebras stress for short periods of time then recover back to their normal state almost immediately (e.g. after running away from a predator). However, in more advanced animal structures, like baboons, where there is a natural pecking order in the group and the animals have too much time on their hands, they can suffer ongoing levels of stress.

Sapolsky speaks of the stress humans suffer, which is often created from our own interpretation of reality. He calls it psychological stress or stress that is the 'invention of our minds', which may not come from a genuine threat.

Often, our stress responses seem (and in most cases probably are) very irrational. Not only do we get stressed in the midst of actual events, but we also get stressed about the possibility that we *may* be confronted by events — however unlikely.

We spend a lot of our time ruminating about what we did or didn't do in the past and we worry about what might befall us in the future. Humans and some primates face severe and prolonged stress caused by psychological or social factors that in no way pose any actual threat to our lives, as would be the case in the wild. We worry about future possibilities, whether real or imagined (e.g. "My business might fail" or "I might stuff up badly"). This is where the power of our mind overwhelms rational thought. We all know we can't change the past; we can only learn from it. We also know that we can't predict the future and have only a very limited ability to affect it. Yet we exhaust huge amounts of energy thinking about it.

☞ *Robert Sapolsky believes we have evolved to be intelligent enough to make ourselves sick with stress.*

We have most control over what we are doing in the exact moment we are doing it. As we expend mental energy ruminating or worrying, we miss what's in front of us. In our business, that could be a solution, an idea, a chance to help a customer or employee, or just enjoying the moment for no other reason than we are alive, well and doing what we love.

What is the result of prolonged stress?

Scientific research by people like Sapolsky and many others has shown that prolonged stress has real and measurable impacts on our health, our life span and our performance. Here are some of the unfortunate realities of prolonged stress:

- neuron damage affecting memory and learning
- reductions in sex drive
- weight gain
- high blood pressure
- coronary heart disease
- sleep loss
- reduced immune function
- vulnerability to depression and other psychological disorders
- damage to unborn foetus
- damage to chromosomes leading to reduced life expectancy.

As you can see by these manifestations of stress, it's not something to treat lightly. It can have severe emotional and physical ramifications if allowed to go on unchecked. In short, it can be deadly.

How can we better manage stress?

Knowing what we now know about stress, how might we better manage stress as we work in our business? Key to this is resilience, which we will discuss a little later on. No single 'cure' is applicable when it comes to stress though. Stress management is a whole-of-life issue and needs to be approached holistically. Stress is also a very individual experience, stemming from past learning, genetics, personality, temperament, our social standing, and our environment. As a result, quick fixes are unlikely.

The following are a few simple things that may knock the edge off your stress while you chip away at longer-term solutions to problems and build your resilience.

First, start accepting that you will face stress. Rather than considering it to be a weakness, spend time becoming comfortable with the idea it will happen and understanding it. You may then be in a better position to manage it.

Here are some questions to reflect upon in times when you feel stressed:

- Do you recognise when you are stressed?
- How do you feel when you are stressed?
- What triggered that particular episode of stress?
- How could you avoid or distance yourself from those triggers?

If the stress comes and goes and you are able to recognise it, there are some important steps you can take to manage them in the short term. Breathe! Stop and take note of the things around you. Bring your mind back to the present moment. These steps can alleviate short-term stressors. Take a look later in this chapter at the further steps you can take to become more mindful.

Are you an optimist or a pessimist?

Some of us are naturally happier and more optimistic. As such, people like that find it easier to weather the blows of life and business. That means some people are naturally more resilient. Those of us (myself included) who are genetically wired to be a little pessimistic and have to work harder to be happy in our business life shouldn't despair. There's also every chance we're beating ourselves up about that pessimistic tendency — a somewhat self-fulfilling and unproductive cycle.

Pessimism, while having a negative connotation, does give us a greater sense of realism in our business.

While becoming more optimistic will take effort, we can make a start. The first step is self-compassion, and the ability to recognise when you start beating yourself up and how you can begin to break that cycle. Managing yourself is about increasing your self-awareness. In this case, accepting that you may not cope as well as others. When you strike a tough situation, accept that you will have to work a little harder to manage it. (This is what Martin Seligman described as Learned Optimism.)

'I don't think I'm any good at this': the business owner's voice of self-doubt

I believe I can say with some confidence that you (and everyone else of sound mind) have had unproductive thoughts at some time in your business life. It can be all too common in business for us to face self-doubt when the cash is tight, when we've lost a customer, when we scolded a staff member or made what proved to be the wrong decision. The good news is you are not alone.

Do any of these thoughts sound familiar?

- I really don't know what I'm doing.
- I feel like an idiot.
- I don't know what to do.
- I'm not smart enough to be doing this.
- Why do those guys find this so much easier than me?
- Why am I having all this bad luck?

And so on.

We all need to show ourselves a little compassion. These thoughts can become 'hooks' that trap us in a pointless cycle. We are human. We will all have these thoughts. The key is to not get stuck on them.

When you experience these periods of self-doubt in business, don't fight the thoughts that come with it. We have little ability to control our thoughts when they come and go. They will come and go continually. The best we can do is accept them, acknowledge them, and even make light of them: "Hey, thanks, mind, but the 'I can't' thoughts aren't very helpful right now!"

Thoughts are not facts. They are not you and they are not necessarily reality. We can't always believe everything we *think*. However, thoughts can have a powerful effect on what we feel and do. All too often, we allow them to roll around in our minds, over and over, potentially reinforcing something that simply isn't true. Yet, fighting them is a fairly fruitless exercise. The more we are able to acknowledge these thoughts, step back from them, let them pass and refocus on what we are doing at that moment, the better chance we have of not being absorbed by them.

Seek the counsel of friends, family and colleagues at times of self-doubt.

How can you become more resilient?

Now that we've discussed stress, optimism, pessimism and happiness, what can you do to enjoy your business journey, not only when everything is going well, but also when it isn't? There's no question that your small business will, at some stage, face difficult times. It is how you handle those challenges that will determine whether you let them rule your life or take greater control of them.

How can you build your physical and mental resilience so that, when faced with a significant business challenge, you are better prepared to cope with it?

Resilience is a process, not a trait. It involves how we interact and negotiate with others, our world, and ourselves. It denotes a way of moving on with a more positive outlook of our business amid adversity, trauma, and everyday pressure.

So how might you increase your resilience when faced with those tougher business challenges?

When faced with adversity, it will trigger past beliefs, which in turn could result in a less-than-helpful response. Our ability to build our resilience gives us a greater chance of responding differently to future adversity.

Our lazy brain

Our brain is a very powerful organ. While it takes up only 2% of our body weight, it uses more energy than any other human organ, accounting for up to 20% of the body's total use. Our brains are also extremely lazy. To conserve energy, our brains will choose the easiest option, the one requiring the least energy. We often choose the easiest answer or option to an issue.

I'm sorry to say that you're wired to take the easiest mental path. Changing the way you behave and approach issues will not come easily and takes a lot of energy. So be kind with yourself. To achieve greater resilience you need to take small measured steps. Be selective on the changes you can realistically make. Reward yourself for small gains. And don't set yourself up to fail by attempting too many changes at once.

Most of all, though, do something! You can't expect a different outcome if you keep doing the same things, as Einstein highlighted in his famous quote.

> *"Insanity: Doing the same thing over and over again and expecting different results."*
> — **Albert Einstein**

Key factors in becoming more resilient

As we've seen, happiness, stress and wellbeing are different for all of us. Therefore, the way to build your resilience in your business will also differ. Considering you can't do it all, focus on the areas in the following list that you believe will help *you* the most.

1. Relationships

Social relationships are vital to our fulfilment and happiness. People who have one or more close friendships are normally happier.

We don't just need relationships; we need *close* relationships. It doesn't seem to matter if we have a large network of close relationships or not. Simply put, it's not the quantity of our relationships but the quality that matters.

These are relationships with people where we are comfortable to share our personal feelings in safety. We can provide them with support and receive support from them. These relationships differ from having a circle of friends where the connections are more superficial. Being part of a large group in a party atmosphere is great fun and we should never underestimate these relationships. However, it is the deep, close relationships that we should nurture and work on most. It is these relationships that will make us more resilient and happier.

During the times you face significant pressures when running your business, you might put your key relationships on hold thinking that you don't have the time to devote to them. Your business is more pressing. Not only does compromising your relationships risk their survival, it in turn makes you unhappy, which will impact your approach to business.

2. Caring for others

Most people who care for others in a selfless manner do so because of a genuine desire to help and improve the world around them. Whether this is volunteer work or simply giving a little extra, the act of caring for others will bring rewards for you.

From a business perspective, this could mean giving back to the community in a way that brings real meaning to you and your business. Caring for others through your business is also likely to be seen in a very positive light by your customers.

A study by the University of Exeter Medical School in the UK compared the physical and mental health of a large group of people who volunteered with a group who did no volunteering. The results showed that the volunteers had fewer instances of depression, greater life satisfaction and a longer life expectancy.

In their research and book *Happy Money*, Elizabeth Dunn and Michael Norton showed that the more money people could give away to others, the happier they became. While I would not suggest you give away your hard-earned dollars freely, this does highlight that the act of giving can make you happier.

3. Physical health

It goes without saying that you are healthier and feel better when you look after your body physically. Healthier people are happier people.

Exercise and diet

The essential part that exercise and diet play in your health is very well documented by a huge array of experts. There's little benefit in my going into detail here. You've probably been badgered about your level of exercise or your less-than-perfect diet at some stage, as we all have, so I'll refrain from forcing greater guilt on you about burning off and restricting the calories.

While I won't write too much on diet and exercise, it doesn't diminish its importance. When you decide on your rules about how you will run your business, do your best to fit in a little exercise and pay attention to what you're eating. It will make you feel better and happier, which will in turn help your business.

Sleep

One other physical health issue critical to building your resilience (and which we too often ignore) is sleep. We are, however, a society that has become very sleep-deprived.

There is a range of scientific views on why the body needs sleep. Russell Foster, Oxford professor and sleep specialist, states that sleep has a vital role in restoration, energy conservation and, most importantly, consolidation of memories and boosting of creativity, areas which are busier when we sleep. Our ability to be more creative and come up with new ideas is enhanced after we have slept compared with when we are tired.

"Sleep is for wimps."
— **Margaret Thatcher**

"Sleep is a criminal waste of time and a heritage from our cave days."
— **Thomas Edison**

Unfortunately, there is an almost perverse view and bravado from people like Thomas Edison and Margaret Thatcher that surviving on little sleep shows great strength. It would seem these people succeeded on very little sleep. Even if that was the case for them, the scientific evidence very clearly disputes this view for most of us.

Sleep is not an indulgence. It is critical for our ability to function, our mental wellbeing and our stress management. The more tired we are, the more stressed we get. We have already discussed the impacts of stress even without a lack of sleep.

Harvard and Berkeley universities carried out a study in 2007. Two groups were tested over a two-day period, one with and one without sleep, using fMRI (functional Magnetic Resonance Imaging) scans to see the impact on the brain. The results showed that sleep deprivation affects our emotional state, can make us irrational, and leads to poor decision-making.

A lack of sleep will directly affect your performance in business. It's very closely correlated to the same drop in performance you get with alcohol consumption. This was proven in studies almost 20 years ago at the Centre for Sleep Research in Australia. Prolonged sleep loss can also have physical health impacts (e.g. increased weight, diabetes).

So how much sleep is enough sleep? The Centre for Sleep Research in Australia states that there are individual differences in each of our responses to sleep loss. (This may even be genetic.) However, if sleep is restricted to fewer than seven hours per night, it will impact function for over 80% of us. Unless you are confident that genetics put you in the 20% group, aim for seven or more hours of sleep every night. What is critical is that you listen to your body. It is likely you will know when you are getting insufficient sleep, whether that's seven or more hours per night.

4. Meaningful work and meaningful goals

Viktor Frankl, in his book *Man's Search for Meaning* about his time in a Jewish concentration camp, put forward a simple but very powerful message. A person can survive almost any situation if they can find meaning in what they do.

While you may never see anything as extreme as Frankl experienced, it highlights the importance of finding a greater meaning in your business if you want to achieve greater happiness.

This is central to the concept of your business having a core purpose. If you have a clear 'why' for what you are doing, you are far more likely to achieve any 'what' you may face.

> *"Everything can be taken from a man but one thing: the last of the human freedoms —*
> *to choose one's attitude in any given set of circumstances, to choose one's own way."*
> — Viktor E. Frankl in *Man's Search for Meaning*

Success for your business, as you define it, should be very much about achieving what brings you meaning. It's about fulfilling your core purpose. No successful business would say that it is motivated solely by financial gain. Financial gain is a natural outcome of a business that is fulfilling its core purpose or true meaning.

At times, you need to ask some fundamental questions about your core purpose in the business and what you define as success. At times, you will pursue success in the eyes of others (climbing the corporate ladder or increasing wealth or status) or gauge your success or lack of it on what others have achieved ("Why can't I be as successful as them?"). It is much easier to lift yourself up from a setback when you are pursuing something you truly believe in and that brings you meaning.

As Einstein stated, "If you judge a fish by its ability to climb a tree, it will live its life believing that it is stupid." If you feel 'stupid' within yourself, perhaps you have not assessed your true purpose or meaning, but are judging yourself by the standards of others.

5. Hold true to your values

It can be very uncomfortable, even stressful, to be in an environment where people claim to work by a certain set of values, yet their behaviours contradict what they purport to believe. For example, "We operate with integrity", yet employees mislead their customers, or "We are respectful" when you see people being treated very poorly. Worse still is a circumstance where you are forced to operate outside your values to run your business.

You may not be aware of these values and therefore struggle to understand why you feel so bad. I will spend some time in later chapters helping you establish what you and your business stand for and what your values are.

Your ability to enjoy the journey in your business will rely heavily on your ability to adhere to your values. In any given situation, it is key to respond in a way that is in line with what is important to you and what you stand for.

6. Keep learning

I'm sure you have experienced the positive feeling associated with learning new skills and the confidence that comes with a deeper understanding of how to manage your business. The fact you're reading this book indicates you want to continue learning.

Until a few years ago, there had been little research to back up what seems, anecdotally, to be clear. Adult learning makes you feel better about yourself, allows you to do more in your life and achieve more in your career. All this has the potential to improve your lifestyle and your wellbeing.

Relatively recently, research has caught up with the anecdotal evidence and revealed that continuous learning helps with goal-setting and creating a sense of achievement. Studies (Aldridge and Lavender in 2000 and John Field in 2008) have shown that continued learning not only benefits us by increasing our employment opportunities, and because of the associated wellbeing that meaningful work brings, but it also increases our:

- self-confidence
- autonomy
- physical health
- capacity to cope with potentially stress-inducing circumstances
- self-esteem
- self-efficacy, or our belief that we will succeed in certain circumstances
- sense of control over our own lives.

Adult learning influences attitudes and behaviours that in turn affect our mental wellbeing.

However, we need to keep some perspective on this. Running off to a course won't necessarily translate into greater meaning in our lives. Like any muscle in our body, our brain is no different in that we need to 'use it or lose it'.

If we add the process of continuous learning through our adult lives, it will only further strengthen our resilience.

7. Staying present and being in the moment

We have made a number of references about managing stress and paralysing thoughts by pausing and refocusing on the present. This is known as being mindful.

Mindfulness is becoming a more widely used term in Western society. It has, however, been part of Eastern cultures for thousands of years. In our world where we are saturated with a huge array of distractions and external stimulation, the moment is often lost. We can start operating on autopilot. Put simply, sometimes we just have to stop and smell the roses.

For those of you who have done meditation or some form of yoga, you will have a strong understanding of the concept of being mindful. However, these pastimes are not everyone's cup of tea. There are still some very simple techniques you can follow to become more present when you feel you are losing control or being overrun with stress or the thoughts rattling around in your head.

Three techniques that Russ Harris suggests in his book *The Happiness Trap* to bring you back to the present moment include:

(i) *Take five breaths*

The breath is a great way to centre you when you are drifting off or feel you are all over the place. You can do it anytime and anywhere.

a. Take five slow, deep breaths. Breathe out as slowly as you can until your lungs are empty. Then let them slowly refill.

b. When you are doing this, focus on your breathing and nothing else.

c. Now look around you and notice what you can see and hear at that point in time.

(ii) *Drop anchor*

This one is aimed at connecting in a simple way with the environment around you. It's particularly good if you are sitting in a room with other people and you feel your stress levels rising.

a. Plant your feet into the floor.
b. Push them down noticing the floor beneath you.
c. Notice the muscle tension in your legs.
d. Now look around you and notice what you can see and hear at that point in time.

(iii) *Notice five things*

This exercise is good if you can briefly escape from your work environment to spend a few minutes in the fresh air.

a. Pause for a moment.
b. Look around you and notice five things you can see.
c. Listen carefully to five things you can hear.
d. Notice anything in contact with your body, like the wind.
e. Now consider all these things impacting on your senses.

The more you do simple little exercises like this, the more they become a habit and the more likely you are to feel in control of your immediate circumstances. Some other simple yet powerful examples to becoming more mindful each day include:

- Pause when you are having that coffee and really taste it.
- Close your eyes when you cuddle your child and really feel what it's like.
- Stop and feel the wind in your face when you walk outside.
- Think about the texture of the food you are eating at lunch.
- Pause from the work at your desk, close your eyes and take two slow deep breaths.

These are techniques that will help snap you out of autopilot, when you switch to it without even knowing it. They will get you focused on what's in front of you and they take only a few seconds.

8. Gaining greater control over your situation

There were two extensive studies carried out to understand health issues in the British civil service, one over a 10-year period from 1967 and one in the late 1990s. These were known as Whitehall Studies. What these studies showed was the further an employee was down the hierarchical ladder, the less control they had over their work environments, caused by a perceived lower social status. This leads to a poorer level of health. These health issues included increased stress, higher levels of heart disease, obesity, and more cases of high blood pressure.

Thankfully, as a business owner, you have less chance of feeling lower on an employment hierarchy. However, if you feel you are not in control of your business circumstances, you are likely to experience the same stress-related issues.

You are more likely to enjoy your business, reduce stress and increase resilience if you feel in control. Gaining greater control of all aspects of your business can be achieved by considering all the aspects discussed later in this book.

Introducing Michelle, the new solo business owner

Throughout the book I will give examples of how you can use the information provided in this book to help your small business. To assist your understanding of how to implement the advice, I've created a fictional small business that will be used to illustrate the point. Michelle's small business is a composite of the many small businesses I have worked with, talked to and read about over the course of my career and in researching this book.

So who is Michelle?

Michelle worked in a middle management role in a mid-size corporate business. She left this business after having her second child. She stayed at home until the two children were well advanced in school, but then found she missed many aspects of work life and wanted to return in some way. She had no desire to get back into middle management or corporate life. She also still wanted to be around home to stay close to her family.

She always had a passion for organic home and hygiene products and would make them for her home, the kids and her husband. She also made them for family and close friends, all of whom raved about how great they were.

Based on this limited market research, she decided to have a go at making some money from selling organic products. If they were popular, she would extend her range of products. She paid for a stall at the local craft market in her rural town to see what happened.

Her first stall was, by chance, just before Christmas and she managed to sell enough of her product to take a little cash home; not to mention the huge satisfaction she got in seeing strangers buy her product and the feeling of achievement to stand up at a stall as a new businesswoman selling something after many years at home.

After speaking to her family and close friends, Michelle decided to take the idea beyond a hobby and see if she could make a business of it.

We will follow Michelle's journey at later stages of the book.

Summary

Most of the improvements you can make for your wellbeing are within your reach. However, I recognise that it may also seem overwhelming at first. I hope you're experiencing good psychological health. While this is less common than we'd like, we can achieve greater wellbeing by recognising that it is a journey and something you will need to work on continually.

Failing to look after your wellbeing is not just a risk to you personally; it's one of the greatest risks to your small business and it's crucial to spend time taking care of it.

To ensure you're moving in the right direction on this journey, keep it simple. Define a *few simple rules* and adhere to them. Let's look at how this might work. Consider what you could do under each of the following headings that will increase your psychological health.

- Spend some time understanding a bit more about yourself, even if that produces some uncomfortable answers.
- Remember that happiness is not about short-term pleasure or contentment. It's about living a rich, full, and meaningful life, which includes the good as well as the bad times.
- We all have a 'happiness baseline' that is determined by genetics but also by our attitude to life. Short-term pleasure or pain does not shift this baseline.
- Your approach to your small business will play a part in your baseline.
- You are human. You will get stressed for what others see as irrational reasons. Don't beat yourself up. Accept your thoughts and don't fight them. You will have thoughts of self-doubt. Be more accepting of these thoughts.
- Understand the values you hold most deeply and consider when they are put under pressure.
- Remember the people who are most special to you. Don't let your business undermine these relationships.
- Show even small amounts of care for others. It helps them and is good for you.
- Do a little exercise and eat just a bit better. Even small efforts will help.
- Try to get a good night's sleep. It's good for you.
- Ask yourself, on the good and bad days, if the business is bringing more meaning to your life than just the money.
- Keep learning. It's good for the business and for you.
- Every now and then stop, take a breath and enjoy that moment. You can't get it back.

⏺ Questions

- How do you define happiness?
- What creates most stress for you in your business?
- How do you establish the times when you feel stressed?
- What techniques do you use to manage your stress?
- What brings you the greatest meaning in your business?
- How well are you sleeping?
- How often do you stop, breathe and enjoy the moment you are in?
- What could you do to increase your resilience?

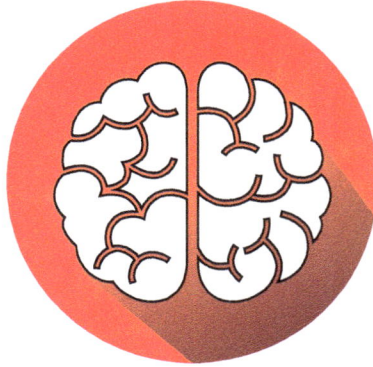

Chapter 3
Getting to Know Your Skills, Personality and Your Limitations

I hope the previous chapter started you thinking more deeply about yourself, what stresses you and what makes you happier. I'd like to take this a little further into your skills, temperament and personality. Many of us find it uncomfortable to consider what we might find if we dig too deep into what makes us tick, but strong self-awareness will only benefit you in your business activities.

Answer the following questions about yourself:

- How clear are you on what you are good at, bad at, enjoy and dislike?
- How well do you understand the effect, good or bad, that you have on the people with whom your business interacts, especially customers?
- Which activities in your business come easiest to you and which take up more energy?
- How comfortable are you to admit your mistakes?
- How comfortable are you to ask for help?
- How would you describe your personality?
- How would you describe your management and leadership style?

Known to Self

OPEN

Things we know about ourselves and others know about us.

Not Known to Self

BLIND

Things others know about us that we do not know.

Hidden Self

HIDDEN

Things we know about ourselves that others do not know.

Unknown Self

UNKNOWN

Things neither we nor others know about us.

Fig. 2: The Johari Window

The Johari Window

The concept of self-knowledge is represented well by the **Johari Window** (Figure 2 above).

The American psychologists Joseph Luft and Harrington Ingham created the Johari Window in 1955. (The name is a combination of the two men's first names.) It is also referred to as the Johari House, with four rooms. It represents a simple perspective on self-knowledge. Ask yourself a few questions about which 'rooms' you have never been in or 'rooms' that others have never been in and how that might be impacting you and your business. How *blind* are you to things others see of you when you are working in your business? What might you be *hiding* from others that you know may be impacting your business? How might you learn about your *unknown self* for the benefit of your business?

Self-knowledge is a lifetime journey. As we age and are exposed to different challenges and events in our lives, we learn more about ourselves. Self-knowledge is a powerful tool that all too many people disregard because it's difficult, uncomfortable or inconvenient to devote time to. The more you can come to grips with this, the more you will enjoy working in your business. You will also be more efficient and have a greater chance of achieving your version of success. So how might you speed up the process of achieving self-knowledge for the benefit of your business? After all, you don't have a lifetime to achieve this for it to be of benefit in your small business.

Consider your circle of competence

Let's start with the most obvious and easiest measurement: the training, experience and skills that you've attained through your business life. We will call this your **competence**.

This may be trade skills, financial or accounting skills, artistic or design skills, sales, marketing or the myriad of skills that small business owners the world over have built up before starting or during their business lifetime.

How competent you are will stand out relative to your competitors. Even if everything else is good about what you do in your business, it's of little use if you are not competent at the core skills required. For example, being a pretty average electrician won't stand you in good stead when going out on your own as an electrician, even if you are exceptional at running the business.

This is the time to be honest. Don't overstate your competencies. Even more importantly, don't understate them. At times, we may lack the confidence to state quite clearly what skills we have. If you're already in business, you may wish to seek out others to provide skills you don't have. The other option is to train in these skills.

If you're looking to branch out into other businesses or buy a new business, be cautious about venturing too far outside your **circle of competence**. Avoid making investments or buying into industries or markets you know nothing about. They may well have a reputation of producing great returns, but if you lack the required skills you are less likely to achieve the success you seek. This is where you need to be brutally honest with yourself about your limitations. Are those limitations something you can fill with external expertise? Is it your heart or your head making the decision?

How can you better understand your personality and temperament?

There is a huge array of techniques used across the world to assist in better understanding our personality preferences, our style and how we interact with others.

Our personality is the sum of all our thoughts, feelings, temperaments, emotions and behaviours that make us unique. Personality arises from within us and remains consistent throughout our life.

Can personality profiling 'tools' help you gain a better understanding of yourself? Personality profiles have been completed by millions of people over many decades. You don't have a lifetime to gain a better understanding of yourself. Some of these techniques may speed up the process.

> *"Learn from the mistakes of others. You can't live long enough to make them all yourself."*
> — **Eleanor Roosevelt**

> *"There is much to be gained by appreciating our differences, and much to be lost by ignoring them or condemning them. But the first step toward seeing others as distinct from yourself is to become acquainted with our own traits of character."*
> — **David Keirsey**, *Please Understand Me II*

Carl Jung — psychological types and personality

Personality theories have been around for almost 100 years. The father of the personality theories is considered to be Carl Jung, a Swiss psychiatrist who released his work *Psychological Types* in 1921. Jung observed that when people's minds are active, they are involved in one of two mental activities. These are:

1. how they take in information (how they perceive things)
2. how they organise that information to make decisions (how they judge things).

He observed two opposite ways you can **perceive** things: either by using our **five senses** or by using our **intuition**. He also described the different ways we prefer to make decisions based on this information. We do this either through **thinking** or through **feeling**, i.e. using our head or our heart. He defined the concepts of **extroversion** and **introversion**. This describes how we are energised either from the outside world or from reflecting within through our thoughts, memories and emotions. The extrovert gains energy from the people around them, from events, activities and the outside world. The introvert gains energy from being by himself or herself, reflecting on their thoughts, feelings and impressions.

> *"Everything that irritates us about others can lead us to a better understanding of ourselves."*
> — **Carl Gustav Jung**

Carl Jung's concepts are now regularly used in mainstream conversation when we describe other people, and have formed the basis of almost every personality profiling technique since then.

Personality profiling tests

You may have heard about a wide range of personality profiling tests you can use to assist in understanding many of the concepts Jung described almost 100 years ago. These tests involve you answering questions that have been refined over many decades to now produce reasonably consistent results.

Tests are widely used by businesses of all sizes throughout the world and may be of interest to you in better understanding how you tick. I will touch on a few of the better-known techniques. The Myers-Briggs Type Indicator (MBTI) and Keirsey's Temperament Sorter are just two of the many tests on offer. A few others I have completed over the years include:

1. The Extended DISC Profile
2. The Dove, Owl, Peacock, Eagle (DOPE) Bird 4 Personality Type Test
3. The Hermann Brain Dominance Instrument (HBDI)
4. The Belbin Team Roles
5. The Team Management Profile Questionnaire — Work Preferences
6. The 5 Dynamics Work Preferences.

Every one of these has assisted in a little greater understanding of myself and the colleagues with whom I took the tests.

Here are a couple of examples in a little more detail that may be of interest.

Myers-Briggs Type Indicator (MBTI)

MBTI was developed by Isabel Briggs Myers and her mother Katharine Cook Briggs in the early 1960s. It was a direct extension of Carl Jung's work. The test is a way to assess how you perceive the world, gather information and make decisions. Personality tests such as MBTI do not measure your intelligence. This test won't tell you what you're passionate about or the state of your mental health. MBTI will assess you on eight characteristics based around Jung's mental activities. How you take in information, how you then make a decision based on that information and whether you are introverted or extroverted.

- Extroversion (E) vs Introversion (I)
- Sensing (S) vs Intuition (N)
- Thinking (T) vs Feeling (F)
- Judgment (J) vs Perception (P)

If you do an MBTI test, you will be identified in terms of four letters (e.g. ESTJ, INTP).

If you gain your energy from the outside world rather than from within, you will be an Extrovert (E). If you prefer to get your information through facts and figures and from what you can touch, see and feel, you will be Sensing (S). If you base your decisions on facts rather than your feelings, then you would be Thinking (T). If you prefer to be well planned, orderly and organised rather than spontaneous and flexible when dealing with the outside world, you would be Judging (J). In this case, your MBTI would be an ESTJ.

It is estimated that each year about 1.5 million people do this test, which is available in over 21 languages. While the results are reasonably consistent, they are not infallible and the process has come under ongoing scientific debate.

Keirsey's Temperament Sorter

Temperament relates to our predisposition to act and interact in certain ways. These are parts of our personality that are innate, that we were born with rather than learned. We often hear mothers say of their children that they were all different from birth. This can be partly attributed to their different temperament.

Temperament and personality are not the same. There are many factors that make up the total personality of a person. Temperament is only one of the many parts that make up your personality.

More recently David Keirsey, an American psychologist, provided greater definition and techniques to measure and use temperaments in a more practical way.

Keirsey believes we can be separated into four main temperaments that he called Artisans, Guardians, Idealists and Rationals.

- **Artisans** are concrete and adaptable. Seeking stimulation and virtuosity, they are concerned with making an impact. They excel at troubleshooting, agility, and the manipulation of tools, instruments, and equipment.
- **Guardians** are concrete and organised. They seek security and want to belong; they are concerned with responsibility and duty.
- **Idealists** are abstract and compassionate. They seek meaning and significance; they are concerned with personal growth and finding their own unique identity.
- **Rationals** are abstract and objective. The seek self-control; they are concerned with their own knowledge and competence. They excel in any kind of logical investigation such as engineering, conceptualising, theorising, and coordinating.

👉 *Do you feel any one of these descriptions of temperament define you more than the others?*

This personality test is well established; over 40 million people have completed Keirsey's Temperament Sorter since it was produced in 1996.

Emotional Intelligence (EQ)

The concept of emotional intelligence rose to dominance in 1995 following Daniel Goleman's book *Emotional Intelligence*. While Goleman was not the first to use the term as we now know it, this title brought it into mainstream conversation.

Goleman argued that our view of intelligence, as defined by the Intelligence Quotient, or IQ, was too narrow and that our emotions play a far greater role in thought and decision-making than was being acknowledged.

Goleman identified the five 'domains' of EQ as:

1. Knowing your emotions
2. Managing your own emotions
3. Motivating you

4. Recognising and understanding other people's emotions
5. Managing relationships.

At the core of emotional intelligence is empathy, or the ability to recognise the emotions and feelings in other people. It's unlikely people will volunteer this information. Those with empathy or strong emotional intelligence are more intuitive to this and better able to engage with these people.

In most personality testing techniques, like MBTI and Keirsey's Temperament Sorter, there are no good or bad answers. They simply recognise your preferences and assist in allowing you to better understand yourself. However, with EQ testing we want to strive for greater emotional intelligence, for greater empathy.

By coming to grips with our level of EQ, we are in a better position to improve on it or at least be more cognisant of the impacts we may have on others if our EQ is lower than we would like.

Putting these tests to use

There is a huge amount of literature and research on the pros and cons of psychological testing. They can be extremely useful in opening you up to aspects of your style, personality and temperament that you might otherwise be blind to. They can be great for sparking discussion within your small team using a common language.

If you wish to do any of these tests, many can be carried out online at little or no cost. The only caution is over-analysing the results and applying them in the wrong way. There is definitely some skill in understanding them at a deeper level.

These tests will never describe everything about you. Yet, they can be a very helpful and fun way to gain another insight into yourself.

We are not always rational decision makers

The normal advice given to small business owners in making the correct decision involves doing some good research, assessing the costs and benefits, removing our emotions, deciding, and then moving on. This sounds very simple and common sense.

However, it is not how we, as humans, interpret information, and then make decisions.

There are decades of research, by people like Nobel Laureate Daniel Kahneman and Dan Ariely, that indicate we do not make decisions this way. In most cases, not only are we irrational in the decisions we make, but also, we are predictably irrational.

The study of the human brain, cognition and psychology continues, and we have so much more to learn, even after decades of research. Understanding some of our mental limitations could assist us as small business owners to make better decisions.

We are confronted with an infinite amount of information throughout our day. The brain must take in this information through our five senses and must filter this information. What poses danger to us is a priority – we act without any analysis when faced with danger. Next priority for our brains is important information that will get our attention (e.g. you always hear your name in a noisy crowd as this is very important to us). What is important to your business is more likely to spark your attention.

Who we are effects our decisions

We have come to this point in our lives, and as business owners, after all our prior years of experience, our education, family, genetics, personality and all those things that make us who we are. We can spend our entire lives learning who we are, what we are good at, what we are weak at, what stresses us and what motivates us. Our decisions are greatly influenced by what makes us who we are so the more we know about ourselves the better will be our decisions.

Our cognitive biases

Because of the huge amount of information we must process, our brains have been trained over our lives to take short-cuts. For example, when we see many faces we sub-consciously decide who poses a threat, which are friendly and which are foe. These short cuts kept our primitive ancestors alive. Unfortunately, these short-cuts lead to biases which may lead to us making incorrect judgments and incorrect decisions. These are a few examples of cognitive biases that effect our decisions:

- Optimism bias — this is highlighted when we say, "that will never happen to me" — chances are it will.
- Confirmation bias — we seek out information to reinforce a well-held belief while we ignore contrary information.
- Loss Aversion — when we compare or weight options, losses loom much larger in our thinking than gains do.
- Framing — we decide differently depending on how information is framed. E.g. While the following two statements mean the same we interpret them differently "You have a 95% chance of a full recovery from this operation" versus "There is a 5% chance you will die".

And there are many more cognitive biases including anchoring, priming, sunk-cost bias, the halo effect, and this is just a sample.

Emotions do play a part

While we would like to think our business decisions are normally rational we can't ignore emotional impacts on our decisions. These are influenced by past experiences, fear, memories and more. There is a growing view by researchers, like Jennifer Lerner, that emotions can improve the quality of our business decisions rather than worsen them.

Gut decisions

There is also a view that intuitive or gut decisions in business may prove more effective than rational well-analysed decisions. Gut decisions are those based on our intuition, with limited analysis. They are usually made very quickly. There is a critical caveat on gut decisions. Those based on deep and detailed experience could be better than those based on analysis. However, if you have no experience you need to be extremely wary about making gut decisions without seeking advice or doing some analysis.

Summary

To recap, take another look at these points that you learned in this chapter:

- The success you define for your small business will relate to the knowledge you have of yourself. Learn as much as you can about this personal side of your business.
- Seek out the blind spots in your self-knowledge.
- Assess your competence honestly. Where are you strong and where else are you weaker?
- Personality tests can help you on the journey of self-discovery. Know what they tell you and accept their limitations.
- Making decisions is critical in your business. However, they may not be rational, may be impacted by biases and emotions.

Questions

- What are you best at?
- What are you worst at?
- What do you most love doing?
- What do you most dislike doing?
- How would you describe your personality and temperament?
- What aspects of your skills and personality do you most wish to focus on?
- How do you approach critical decisions that you must make about your business?

Chapter 4
What is Your Strategy?

The word 'strategy' is too often seen as the domain of the military or big business. Frequently, it is looked upon with a dose of scepticism from small businesses. However, I am of the strong belief that a strategy is just as vital for you as it is for any business.

The *Oxford English Dictionary* defines 'strategy' as:

A plan of action designed to achieve a long-term or overall aim.

The concept of strategy was born out of the military. The word comes from its French (*stratégie)* and Greek (*stratēgia*) origins, meaning 'lead' or 'generalship'.

The word 'strategy' became commonly used during the Napoleonic Wars. People like Carl von Clausewitz, who studied Napoleon and his strategies of war, are often credited with its use. The concept has been around for much longer if one considers Sun Tzu's 500 BC *The Art of War*. It only became common in the language of business in the 1950s and '60s.

Willie Pietersen's definition of strategy, as it relates to business, is one of the simplest and most compelling I have come across.

"What gave birth to strategy was the need to respond to two inescapable realities: the fact that we have limited resources, and the inevitability of competition."
— Willie Pietersen, Columbia University

It further demonstrates how strategy is as relevant to small businesses as it is to big business. No matter how big a business is, it never has unlimited resources. It must make choices: firstly, what it **will do** to be successful; and even more importantly, what it **won't do**.

Every business exists to meet the needs of someone. Even not-for-profits, charities, monopolies and government departments serve the needs of someone. If they don't meet these needs as well as an alternative option or competitor, those they serve will go elsewhere. So the process to develop your small business strategy needs to answer two key questions:

1. *What will you do and what won't you do now and in the future to achieve the success you seek from your business?*
2. *Who are your customers and how do you serve them?*

I believe the need for a small business to develop strategy will only become more critical as the world becomes ever smaller, more sophisticated and more competitive.

Small businesses often don't take a long-term view; they have no strategy, no business plan, no exit or succession plan. They see strategy as the domain of big business when it can be brief and simple.

Strategy should address some simple questions:

- "Why does your business exist?" (your purpose)
- "What does your business stand for?" (your values)
- "Where do you want your business to be in three to five years?" (your goals)

What are the consequences of ignoring strategy?

Far too many small businesses fail while similar large businesses live on. There are many reasons for this. One is that small businesses don't set aside enough time or put enough priority on their future. They lose sight of why they got into business or of external pressures that may shut them down. While larger businesses have the resources to monitor the external world, develop and then execute strategy, it is no less critical for a small business. It could be argued that it is even more critical to small businesses as they are less able to survive the external shocks that a large business can tolerate.

> *"Out there in some garage is an entrepreneur who's forging a bullet with your company's name on it."*
> — Gary Hamel, business writer

There may well be an entrepreneur forging a bullet with your company's name on it. You may be the entrepreneur forging the bullet. Or maybe both.

Why does your business exist?

The *reasons* we go into owning our own business will be varied. You may have been in a small business your entire working life. You could have been handed the business from your family. You might have wanted a lifestyle change. You may have an idea that you believe has huge potential. You possibly bought a business. Or you may just not want to work for anyone else any more. Whatever the circumstances for going into your small business, there will be a core reason that drove you to be in this position. Sometimes, we enter the small business world with well-meant but misguided intentions. Perhaps if we knew what we know now we may never have done it.

It is not that hard to set up a business. You had an idea, a passion, a love or you simply wanted the freedom that small business offers. But you may have found the work born out of love becomes a chore requiring you to use less familiar or less enjoyable skills. You might even be earning much less than you thought and usually working much harder. Before you get into the more specific aspects of your business, answer the following questions:

- What does your business offer you besides making a living?
- What gap (no matter how small) would arise if your business no longer existed?
- Why is your small business's existence important to the people you currently or want to serve?

When you started your business, did you quickly find you were focused solely on getting it off the ground? Once you got it up and running, did you have to work even harder to keep things going? If it feels hard, it might mean you've lost sight of the most critical aspects of being in business:

- *Why* does it exist?
- *Why* did you start it?
- *What* purpose does it fulfil?
- *What* meaning does it bring you?

> *"Purpose is what gives life meaning."*
> — C.H. Parkhurst, American clergyman and social reformer

In answering these questions, you are defining what many organisations describe as their **Core Purpose**.

☞ *Your ability to prosper as a business is not just determined by what you sell. It is far more about what you believe, how your customers look upon you and what value you bring to them. If you are unable to establish your core purpose, it's unlikely customers will understand it either.*

Examples:

Tourism New Zealand

☞ "100% PURE NEW ZEALAND"

Disney

☞ "TO MAKE PEOPLE HAPPY"

XERO

☞ "TO MAKE SMALL BUSINESSES MORE PRODUCTIVE"

World Vision

☞ "OUR VISION FOR EVERY CHILD —LIFE IN ALL ITS FULLNESS; OUR PRAYER FOR EVERY HEART —THE WILL TO MAKE IT SO."

Your small business's core purpose is the reason it exists. Do you know the reason your business exists? Why did you start it? Is that reason as strong now as it was then?

You may say it exists to make you a living. However, there are probably many easier ways you could make a living than owning a small business. Besides, why would your customers care about the money you want to make. Owning your own business can become all-consuming. If you are not clear **why** it exists, **what** meaning you hope to gain from it, then it is unlikely you will last for long.

If making a living or creating a job is your business's core purpose, you will soon run out of energy and your customers will see your business for what it is — a job for you.

If you really look at your business and your motives, I doubt that money alone is your core purpose. Money is a necessary outcome of a successful small business. It is not the sole purpose it exists.

It is the core purpose that also inspires and continues to motivate you, your business partners, your associates and your employees (if you have any).

So, what is your business's core purpose?

☞ *Avoid those waffly, vague (and therefore meaningless) vision and mission statements that many larger organisations trap themselves into writing. If you don't genuinely believe in your core purpose, don't write it down and definitely don't advertise it. It will only serve to demotivate you and confuse your customers.*

The power of SWOT

I'm a big believer in not reinventing the wheel, if a really good and simple business process already exists. One such process, to assist in prioritising and formulating your strategy, is SWOT (strengths, weaknesses, opportunities and threats). Even to the uninitiated, it is probably a term you have heard. Due to its overuse in the corporate world, though, SWOT has copped a bad rap. Despite its image, it is still one of the most powerful tools to help execute strategy and a great tool for the small business owner.

There is some debate over who first came up with the concept. However, Albert Humphrey is most often credited with the idea. He led a research project at Stanford University in the 1960s and '70s using data from many companies. The goal was to identify why corporate planning failed. The resulting research identified a number of key areas of failure, and the tool used to explore each of the critical areas was an initial form of what is now called a SWOT analysis.

Face your 'brutal realities'

Your business could face some brutal realities, both from within the business and externally to the business. However, this should not be at the expense of remaining positive about the future, and maintaining the conviction to persist and achieve your goals.

I don't believe anyone has put forward a more powerful statement covering the balance between maintaining a positive attitude in the face of brutal realities than Admiral James Stockdale. He survived seven years in a Vietnamese prisoner of war camp.

> The Stockdale Paradox
> *"You must never confuse faith that you will prevail in the end — which you can never afford to lose — with the discipline to confront the most brutal facts of your current reality, whatever they might be."*
> — **Admiral James Stockdale**

While you won't face the same brutal facts as Stockdale, you will need to consider the reality of your business's circumstances, both good and bad. You need to maintain a positive view of the future and then get on with it.

When completing your SWOT be honest about your circumstances, including the brutal facts.

Your internal focus

You first need to look within your business. In SWOT, the internal analysis considers your business's **strengths** and **weaknesses**. We have already touched on this for you personally. It's now time to look at the business.

- What strengths does your business possess that will help you deliver on your goals?
- What weaknesses are most likely to impede your progress?

This is the time to be brutally honest with yourself, which means not only accepting your weaknesses, but also not underselling your strengths. It may help to get a colleague or an advisor that knows you well to challenge you on some of these. You don't need a friend who is going to be nice to you. In business, NICE translates to *Not Interested to Care Enough*! You don't need nice people when doing this process.

Your external analysis

There will be much going on in the outside world that will provide opportunities for your small business. However, there will also be just as many things that will trip you up if you don't see them coming. We summarise these as **opportunities** that exist now or in the future in the world outside the business and **threats** external to the business that could have a serious impact .

As you can well imagine, you could be overloaded dealing with the breadth of information outside your small business, especially given how small the world is today. Let's look at another proven and simple method to filter this information and prioritise the actions stemming from your review of the external world.

Porter's Five Forces

Michael Porter introduced his concept of the five competitive forces in his book published in 1980. Since then, it has been quoted and used extensively around the world. Let's break it down and see how you could apply it (see Figure 3 below).

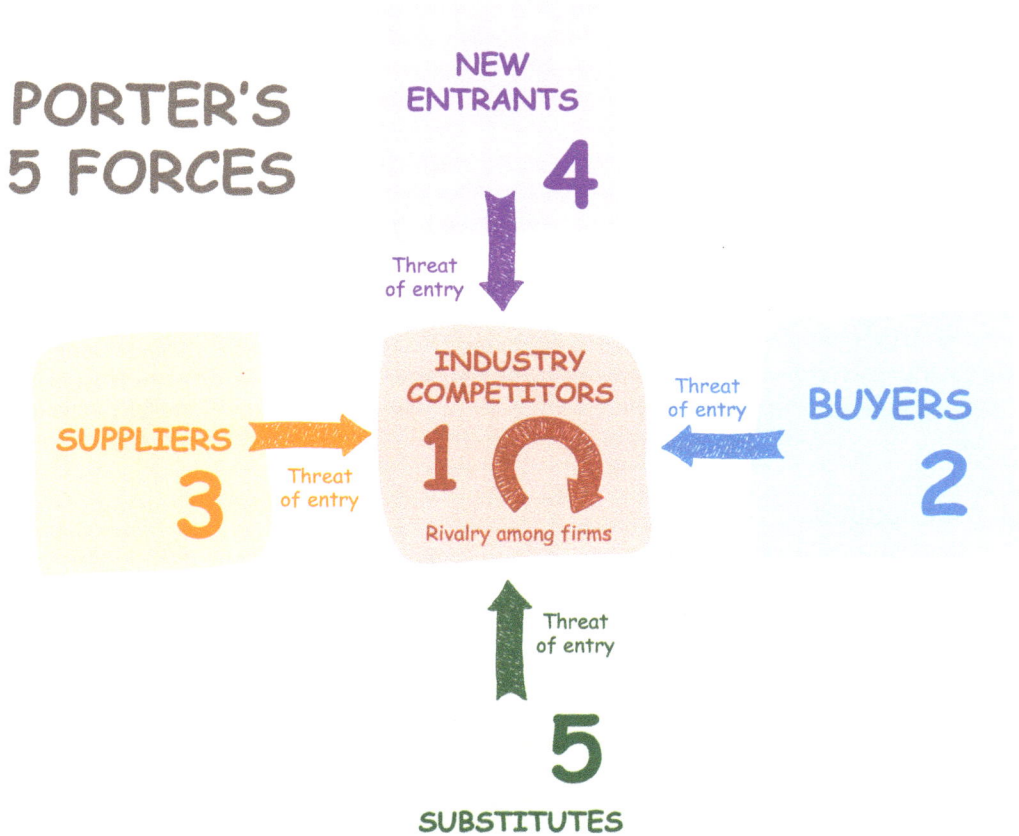

PORTER'S 5 FORCES

NEW ENTRANTS

4

Threat of entry

INDUSTRY COMPETITORS

1

Rivalry among firms

SUPPLIERS

3

Threat of entry

Threat of entry

BUYERS

2

Threat of entry

5

SUBSTITUTES

Fig. 3: Porter's Five Forces

1. Existing competitors

As a small business, you are likely to have many competing companies, most much bigger than you. While your competitors should not overawe you, it is worth understanding who they are, what they are doing and what you might learn from them.

Understanding the following points could prove invaluable:

- What is their point of difference?
- What marketing are they doing and do you like it?

- How much are they charging for their products and services?
- What part of their business could you learn from and use in a way that aligns with your purpose, values and goals?

> *"Immature poets imitate; mature poets steal."*
> — T.S. Eliot

There are no prizes in business for coming up with the newest idea. Very rarely is any idea completely new. It is usually influenced by what someone else has already done. If someone else is doing something really well, learn from them.

2. Your customers

We will discuss more about identifying and engaging with your ideal customers when we get into marketing in later chapters. For now, it is worth considering the risks and opportunities your customers may pose. For example, are you reliant on a small number of powerful customers?

3. Your suppliers

It is very likely you'll have a range of suppliers from whom you buy products or services. Given your size, you probably don't have much influence over those larger suppliers and it's more likely they will be able to impact you seriously. If these suppliers raise their prices, for example, alter their quality, cease to offer a product you rely on, or alter their service levels in any way, you may find yourself stranded. Look to those suppliers who could hurt you the most and consider what you would do if they fail to deliver what you want. It is rare that there would be absolutely no other option at your disposal. If there isn't, you will need to look at what you'll do if that supplier backs you into a corner.

4. New entrants

There is every chance new people could come into your marketplace and directly compete with you. As we discussed earlier, it's easy to open a small business. The barriers for similar competitors entering your marketplace could be quite low. If you are doing really well, it's likely someone else will see this and want a piece of your action. Some new business may enter your market simply because they want to start a business for lifestyle reasons, having done no research and not realising that the market may already be overcrowded. You may get no warning about new entrants. The key will be to maintain a level of oversight of your marketplace and be nimble enough to respond. The other critical point to remember is that, if you have loyal customers, they are unlikely to jump ship because someone else pops up.

5. Substitutes

This relates to products or services that come out and make your offering redundant. You may be well aware of the existing competition for your product or services and comfortable you can compete. You may also be comfortable that you could survive a couple of new entrants. However, can you survive a business coming into the market that sells products or services that make yours redundant? An example of this was with a husband and wife who ran a business processing photographs from negatives in a mid-size town. They had borrowed to purchase their equipment and they faced little competition in the area when they started. Regrettably, they underestimated the interest in digital photography and, before they could adjust their business, their sales plummeted and did not allow them the financial capacity to change. They went out of business, taking with them a large debt.

Other external factors not covered by Porter

Porter's Five Forces do not consider some other key issues. Let's touch on these briefly.

Political or regulatory changes

Governments at all levels of the political spectrum come and go. With this comes regulatory and legal changes that could see your business boom or disappear. They could just make business harder than it needs to be. As a small business owner, you are unlikely to have any political influence at all. For example, the Tech Lobby spends about $US 100 million per year in Washington DC. The British financial services industry spends more than £90 million per year on lobbying. Neither gets what it wants all of the time. On this basis, I doubt small business owners stand much of a chance at having any political impact.

This does not mean you should do nothing. If your business has access to industry associations, look to join them. They may lobby on behalf of their members. If not, they may at least be aware of potential changes in the law ahead of time. If you rely heavily on government policies to attract revenue, consider the impact of potential changes.

Technological changes

The ongoing changes in technology could offer significant benefits or threats to your business.

Economic and social changes

Downturns in the economy or changes in social preferences could provide great opportunities or threats depending on your business. Again, you will have limited ability to influence these but staying abreast of what is happening around you will better prepare you.

Pulling together your SWOT

After walking through all these points, I'm sure you'll have a much better understanding of your small business. I'm also hopeful that many thoughts are coming to you regarding all the factors that may impact on you from your external world, as either opportunities or threats. If not, spend a few hours in the newspapers, searching the web, and look in industry newsletters and magazines to see if anything springs to mind. To establish your strengths, weaknesses, opportunities and threats, work your way through the following points. It is even more effective if you can carry this out with someone else.

1. Put down the four SWOT headings (strengths, weaknesses, opportunities and threats) on a sheet of paper.
2. Write down every idea that comes into your head under each heading. Keep going until you run out of ideas. Don't analyse or edit just yet.
3. Take a break, then come back and start grouping similar ideas together.
4. You don't need to do much more with your strengths. Note what they are and keep using them. However, our focus is now on the weaknesses, opportunities and threats.
5. Develop a single list with all the grouped items from the weaknesses, opportunities and threats above.
6. Now reduce that list to (strictly) just your top five items only.
7. Don't lose any of this information. It's too valuable to lose. What isn't a priority now may rise to the surface later.

You should now focus on these **five priorites**.

Let's use Michelle's business and her recent goal of growth to see how the SWOT method can be used in a small business.

Michelle's SWOT

Goals
- To be a supplier of eco-friendly body products into retail stores and online.
- To increase turnover (revenue) to $300,000 by the end of three years.
- To increase the product range to meet more customers' needs.

Internal to Her Business

Strengths	Weaknesses
- Passionate about the venture. - Skilled in making unique soaps. - Very low fixed costs. - Cheaper than similar soaps in retail shops. - She has a very creative mind and boundless ideas.	- She hates the finance and admin work. - She has no systems in place. - Limited inventory of stock if demand increases. - Not known outside local groups. - Little available cash at present to deliver on the abundance of ideas. - Only one product available to sell. - No brand awareness. - Can't quite define her ideal customers. - Not crystal clear on her point of difference.

External to Her Business

Opportunities

- Gap in the market for her organic soaps.
- Sell into local retail shops.
- Most soaps in this market are not organic.
- Develop a niche for eco-soaps through entire product life cycle.
- Extend into other organic body products and cosmetics.
- Develop an eco-charity to support branding.
- Online sales targeting a specific niche for high-end, quality eco body products.

Threats

- Only one supplier in town for raw material.
- Online sale of soaps from Asia.
- The company 'Eco Soap Inc.' is marketing new organic soaps in local stores.
- Possible regulations on requirements for eco branding have been mentioned.

Michelle's Key Priorities

SWOT Summary

Top Five Issues

1. Lack of funding for inventory and new equipment.
2. Lack of product awareness outside local community.
3. Not enough product choices to meet demand.
4. Consideration of how to take advantage of the significant interest for these products in this niche.
5. Not enough testing of the market to establish demand for different products (and the need to get help with administration).

Summary

Some closing thoughts on strategy:

- Strategy involves managing a business's limited resources and its relationships with those it serves. This is as relevant to a small business as a large corporation or an army.
- Be clear on why your small business exists and what its core purpose is. You will have days where you ask yourself "Why am I doing this?" It's good to have a clear answer to that question.
- Establish your SWOT — Your internal strengths and weaknesses and the external opportunities your business has and the external threats it may face.
- Be careful not to set too many priorities. About five strategic objectives each year should suffice.
- Porters Five Forces may help establish your SWOT.

Questions

- Why does your business exist — what is its core purpose?
- How will customers relate to this purpose?
- How clear are you on your business's strengths and weaknesses?
- What opportunities and threats exist for your business?

Chapter 5
Executing Your Strategy

We have now discussed the importance are formulating a strategy for your small business. This will mean little if you are unable to execute that strategy. As you work your way through the remaining chapters of this book start thinking about how you will finalise the strategy for your business but, more importantly, how you will bring that strategy to life.

As we discussed, strategy is to help you make choices. To establish what you will do and what you won't do. The SWOT analysis will have assisted in establishing your strengths, drawing out the weaknesses you need to consider, the threats that may de-rail you, and the opportunities you want to pursue However, you will continue to be faced with many priorities, many choices and many different paths you and your business could take. This could become overwhelming, especially with your limited resources.

Let's spend some time discussing the challenge of having too much to do and too little time before looking at how to manage it.

Cognitive overload, cognitive capacity and too many choices

Our cognitive capacity

All human beings have a limit to their cognitive capacity to take in information and process it. **Cognition** is a general term covering our mental processes, including attention, memory, language and knowledge.

George Miller, one of the founders of cognitive psychology, wanted to understand what the limits were on our capacity to process and then remember information. In 1956, he quantified our capacity in the paper 'The Magical Number Seven, Plus or Minus Two'.

He performed a number of tests where he asked his subjects to pay attention to a number of items, retain them, and then repeat back what they could remember. He kept finding that across a wide range of tasks the number seven kept popping up as a limit on human performance. His article established that the limit to our information processing was seven items, plus or minus two; that is, some of us may manage nine and some of us only five, but on average it's seven.

In short, realise that, when you are confronted with a huge number of choices and new information, you, like every other person, will be limited in how much of this data you can take in and process.

Cognitive overload

George Miller also pioneered work on **cognitive overload**. Your working memory (or short-term memory) has limited capacity. Attention, described in psychology as the process allowing us to enhance some information and block out other information at any given moment, is also limited.

If confronted with too much information (for example, constant requirements to multi-task) and/or being interrupted continually, this could lead to cognitive overload. If this occurs, we make more mistakes, stop paying attention to critical information, and our ability to learn diminishes. Also, we fail to commit as many thoughts to memory. If you add to this increased stress, lack of sleep, or worse still drugs and alcohol, you can probably guess how effective you are going to be.

If, however, you have built up a wealth of knowledge and experience, your mind will be effectively pre-trained to identify these issues and you can quickly choose the best option. In this case, it is your subconscious that kicks in.

In another perspective from the book *Outliers*, Malcolm Gladwell put forward the view that true expertise comes with 10,000 hours of practice (up to five years doing nothing else). If you have this much practice or experience, you may be able to manage the breadth of information your new business will face. You will be better placed to ignore anything irrelevant and focus on the key factors.

If you are inexperienced, your capacity is limited. You are not slow. You are just human.

The Jam Experiment and choosing

In her book *The Art of Choosing*, Sheena Iyengar outlined her research on how people make choices and what impacts on the quality of those choices. She carried out wide research. One of her simple experiments was carried out in a large US-based delicatessen called Draeger's. Draeger's exists in a number of US cities. The store offers a huge variety of products. For example, it offers 15 types of bottled water, 150 types of vinegar, 250 types of cheeses, 300 flavours of jam, and much more. Such choice was one of their points of difference, of which they were very proud. This created a lot of consumer interest and attracted a lot of people to their stores. Iyengar's research set out to determine whether this level of choice actually translated into sales.

Iyengar instructed her team to set up a tasting stall for the jams near the storefront. In the first test, there were almost 30 flavours that customers could choose to sample. This large selection attracted most of the people who entered the store. They were asked to taste as many jams as they could. They typically stopped tasting after only two jams. If they liked a jam they could go to the store shelves and buy their selection from the 300 flavours at a healthy discount. Unfortunately, most got to the jam shelves, became confused, and debated the merits of a choice for up to 10 minutes. Less than 5% ended up buying anything.

In the second test, there were only six jams that customers could choose to taste. In this case, customers again still only tasted two jams. However, when confronted with the large selection, they were far more confident in their final choice, selecting it almost immediately. Of the customers who had to choose from six, 30% made a purchase and were also completely comfortable with that choice when interviewed later.

While Draeger's continued with their strategy, because it attracted huge numbers of people, they had to assist customers in narrowing their choices in order to convert the browsing into sales.

As demonstrated, we love to be offered a huge choice; in fact, we find it fascinating. However, if confronted with too much choice, we feel obliged to devote greater time to the choice and either decide not to choose because it's too hard, or are left with an uneasy feeling that we made the wrong choice, even if the choice met our needs.

> *"When people are given a moderate number of options (4 to 6) rather than a large number (20 to 30), they are more likely to make a choice, are more confident in their decisions, and are happier with what they choose."*
> — **Sheena Iyengar,** *The Art of Choosing*

Filter and prioritise choices

Now, you know you're not superhuman. You can't remember everything. You can't process everything. To improve the quality of your choices, you need to simplify and reduce those choices to a manageable number.

In short, in executing your strategy and goals, **you must prioritise!**

Before you start launching into the next steps of the 'doing', you need to take your newfound knowledge and start assessing what your priorities are in the next three to six months, then out to the next 12 months, with your sights on your three- to five-year goal, which we will discuss shortly. These priorities will be impacted by the internal limitations of your small business (including you) and the external factors that are bearing down on you.

You need to allocate some time to set your goals, values, strategy and plans. Block out a day or two, disappear from the day-to-day grind and focus on you and your bigger picture priorities. If you don't do this, **nothing will change!**

Planning — Executing your priorities

Here's where business owners can fall down. You must execute your priorities. You alone can make them happen.

This is when the rubber hits the road. It is of little use having great inspirational goals, developing a very good strategy and a strong list of priorities if they collect dust in the corner of your office.

The execution is where most strategies and long-term plans tend to disintegrate, but it's the perfect time to not follow the lead of large organisations in that sense. In a report by SAS Business Analytics that measured the execution of strategy, a staggering 90% of companies fail to execute their strategies after developing them.

It's critical at this stage to ask yourself where your time is best spent. Being an Under 5 will bring with it the temptation to do everything. Occasionally, you should ask yourself where in your business the next hour of your time would bring most value. Is it trying to fix the computer or chasing a strong lead? Is it writing that blog article or reconciling the receipts? Is it a coffee with a new customer or reading the monthly financial report?

All these must happen, but you can't do them all, all the time. Do what adds most *value* to the business and what will set you on the path to achieving your goals.

✔ Develop your Strategic Plan

A strategic plan (also called a business plan) adds specific targets and deliverables you wish to pursue. Typically, it involves no more than 12 months of operation and often it aligns with the time you must close out your accounts for the tax year. It will outline the goals for your business and your core values, as we will discuss in the next few chapters. It should also cover the key priorities .

Businesses tend to over-complicate the business planning process, but it can be simple. In fact, I believe it should be no more than a page of words plus a page showing your budget, which we cover in later chapters. It should remain dynamic rather than a large document that collects dust. It should also be visible, so you and your staff can continue to gauge where you are on the journey and whether the journey is taking you in the right direction.

You can personalise this any way that works for you. However, you need to write it all down and continue to refer to it.

Key performance indicators

This term is used very commonly in large businesses to explain the measures you will monitor closely. Whatever you choose to keep an eye on must be measurable and truly reflect what must happen to stay on track. This must be combined with a clear quantitative target that you are attempting to meet.

Typical examples are:

- Monthly sales volumes will exceed 100 units.

- Monthly revenue will exceed $ 2,000.
- We will return 100% of all customer calls within 24 hours.
- Our monthly cash in the bank will increase by $ 1,000/month.

And so on.

See the Strategic Plan template you can complete at the back of the book.

Summary

Key considerations for setting your priorities after you have clarity on your strategy, goals, marketing and staffing include the following:

- Start developing your Strategic Plan.
- One of the key concepts of strategy is that you will have many more things to consider doing than your capacity will allow, so choose which you will prioritise.
- You have the same physiological limitations we all have. You have limited cognitive capabilities to manage too many tasks at once. The quality of your choices may be compromised if you have too much on your plate.
- Be careful not to set too many priorities. About five strategic objectives each year should suffice.
- Execute well through good planning (e.g. weekly, monthly and yearly plans).
- Track your performance.
- Time is your enemy. No-one can give you more hours. Set aside time to get out of the chaos and ponder where you are on your journey and where you are heading.

Questions

- What five priorities in the next year will most contribute to achieving your goals?
- What are the priorities for your business over the next three months?

Chapter 6
What Do You and Your Business Stand For — Your Values?

In business, you will rarely have a set of prescribed ways to behave or react in different situations. You will have to make decisions with limited information. To do this, you need something to guide you on this journey, so you can make the best decisions at the time, especially when those decisions are really challenging.

> "The greatest help in meeting any problem with whatever courage is demanded is to know where you yourself stand. That is to have in words what you believe and are acting from."
>
> — **William Faulkner, American writer and Nobel laureate**

You need to understand what your business stands for. When your customers, your staff and others hear about you, what will spring into their mind? What is the moral compass that will guide you and your business?

What you and your business stand for is often described in your **values**.

The *Oxford English Dictionary* defines 'values' as:

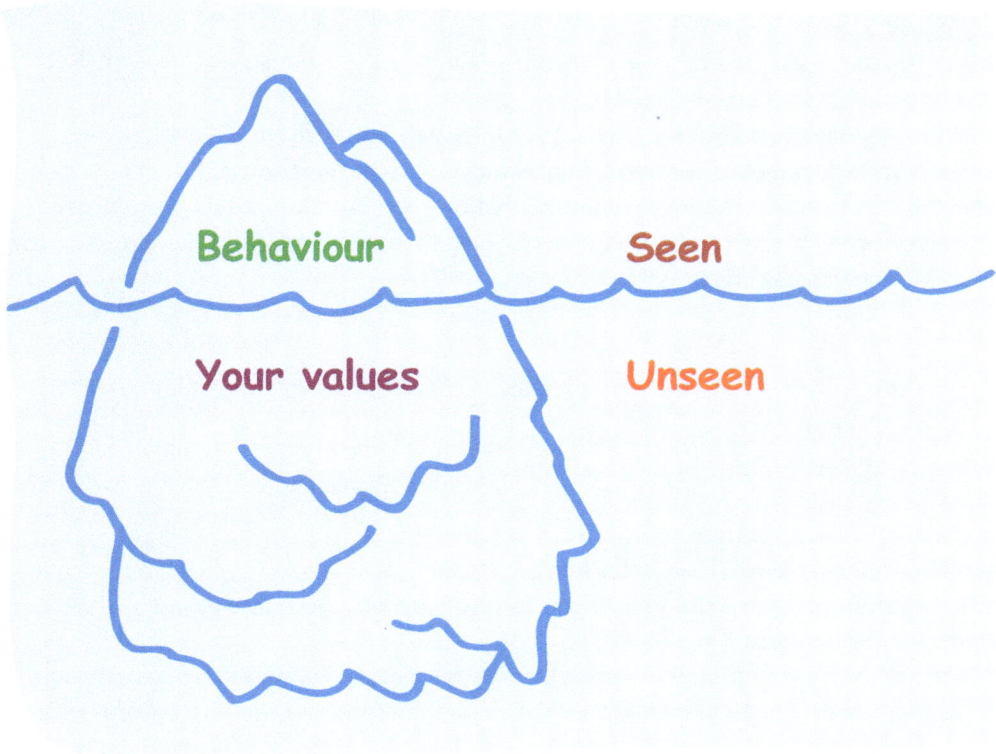

Behaviour — Seen

Your values — Unseen

Principles or standards of behaviour; one's judgment of what is important in life.

Values are the standards or principles that have a major influence on your thinking and behaviours. Often, the times we feel at our best are the times when we are living in accordance with our values. Values do not just relate to you in your personal life. The values of your small business will strongly reflect your own values.

The window into your values is through your behaviours, as these will be what your customers, employees and suppliers see. Decisions to buy from you, sell to you or work for you may be greatly influenced by the values you display. If your behaviours are inconsistent with your stated values, your authenticity will be brought into serious question.

It is very important that you take time to understand and accept your values. This is not just some abstract, feel-good concept. Nor is it only the domain of big business. If you don't know what your business stands for, what will set you apart from anyone else? Why should customers become loyal to you if the basis of your business is superficial?

Values are not goals. Goals can change throughout the life of your business. Goals are something you can reach, tick off as you complete them, then set new ones. These goals may or may not be consistent with our values. For example, 'to be loved' is a goal, yet 'to be a loving person' is a value. Goals are time-bound, whereas values are ongoing.

Values are not feelings either, although we tend to 'feel' better when we are acting in accordance with our values.

We could have a very wide range of values that we fall back on in different situations. Our values can evolve and change as we grow. Our values as a pre-school child are likely to be different from those we would have as a parent.

What you need to do is narrow in on your **Core Values**. These are the three to five values that stand out from all others. They are what you will never waver from no matter what the circumstance. You may not know what they are, but they exist within you even if you have not established them yet. Understanding them will help you achieve the success you seek in your small business.

> *"Values aren't buses . . . They're not supposed to get you anywhere. They're supposed to define who you are."*
> — Jennifer Crusie, author

What are your personal values?

Let's walk through an exercise to help you narrow in on what your core values are. Use this simple exercise to assist.

Scribble down your thoughts when you do this exercise. Writing them down will help clarify them, allow you to more easily sort through them, and provide a list you can refer back to at a later time.

Exercise

Consider a time in your working life when you felt at your worst due to circumstances within the work environment.

- What were you feeling?
- What was happening at that time?
- How were you being treated?
- How were people around you being treated?
- What words best describe this situation?

Consider a time in your working life when you felt at your best due to circumstances within the work environment.

- Ask yourself the same questions.

Write down the individual words that best describe what comes to mind in these examples. These will be words like courage, honesty, joy, warmth, creativity, care, accountability, commitment, decisiveness, initiative, strength, service and excellence.

You may come up with a long list to start with. Try to narrow these down to three to five words that represent the values you hold most strongly.

What are your business values?

Now that you have some greater clarity on your personal values, narrow in on your business values. If you were asked how you wanted customers to describe your business in a word, what would you want them to say? Would it be courageous, caring, friendly, competent, authentic, innovative, creative, disciplined, detailed or competitive?

As with your personal values exercise, list all the words that represent what you believe your business stands for. Then reduce them down to three to five. There will almost certainly be some alignment between your personal and business values.

Convert values to business behaviours

Too often, businesses leave the process there. This is especially true in large corporations. While you will know exactly what you mean when you use one of these words, most people around you, especially your customers, won't. You need to convert these words into a statement that reflects the behaviours that people will see when you are living these values. Use your own words and don't get too hung up on finessing the language.

Here are a few examples from a range of businesses that I've picked up over time:

- "We don't do dirty" — an air-conditioning installation business on their value of cleanliness.
- "We will have fun" — a US airline for on-board attendants.
- "Promise them everything, give them more" — a painter-decorator.
- "Be accurate" — a rural legal business.
- "Tell clients what's happening" — the same legal business.
- "Yes we can" — a truck repair and maintenance business.

The key point is that you choose the values that are real for you and that you genuinely believe. If you are just going through the motions and you know you'll let those values slip when times are tough, then writing them up will do you more harm than good.

Just remember, you and your business will have a set of values whether you articulate them or not. People will determine what they believe they are through your behaviours and actions.

Summary

Here are a few of the key points to follow up from this chapter:

- You and your small business have a set of values whether you are clear on what they are or not.
- People will assess what your values are based on your behaviours and your actions, not on what you say.
- Spending time to determine your values will guide you in your decisions, set standards for any employees and grow your small business brand.
- There are some simple exercises you can do to gain initial insight into your values.
- If you want to use your values more openly, use language that reflects actions to which you, your staff and your customers can relate.

Questions

- What are your three to five core values that you will never compromise in running your business?
- What behaviours will you and your staff demonstrate if you are all acting consistently with these values?
- What actions would you take if you saw people in your business acting contrary to these values?

Chapter 7
What Are the long-term Goals for Your Business?

Where do you want your business to be in three to five years (and beyond)?

A key part of the development of strategy is the long-term goal for your business. You need to ask yourself:

- What do I want to get out of my business?
- I know why I started my business, but where do I want it to go now?
- What is success for me?
- Knowing what I know now, what would my business be doing in three to five years' time?

From this goal, you can work back to a one-year and then even closer to, say, the next three months to define shorter-term targets and goals. Without a longer-term goal, you will simply be drifting along as the years fly past.

In a rapidly moving world, goals will need to be reviewed and strategic shifts may be required as the years pass. This can be assessed throughout the journey as part of future strategy development and goal-setting, which are never static processes.

A word of caution. You want realistic achievable goals, not pipedreams or wishes. By all means stretch yourself. Make your goal audacious if necessary. However, be cautious of setting yourself up for failure. If you can see a line-of-sight from your three-month and one-year goals to your long-term goals then you are on your way. If opportunities present themselves on the journey and these accelerate achieving (or surpassing) your goals, that's fantastic. If your goals are measurable and specific rather than vague, then you'll be confident of reaching them.

Generic business goals

While all businesses are unique, the strategies that many small businesses pursue are likely to be covered by one of many generic goals. These generic goals are a helpful starting point to help you define your own. You may decide your goals are a combination of these generic goals. And that's great.

No single generic goal can be looked upon as being more or less successful than the other. You decide what goal fits your needs at that time in your business's life.

Further to this, I believe that every person entering a business should have at least some idea about how they will exit the business. That is: you should have the end in mind at the beginning of the business's life. Yes, your views will change or other opportunities could arise. As mentioned, strategy and goal-setting are not static processes. Perhaps Mike Tyson explained how circumstances often shift your strategy and goals:

> *"Everybody has a plan until they get punched in the mouth."*
> — Mike Tyson

So yes, your plans or goals may cop a punch in the mouth along the way, but you have to start with some sense of where you want your business to head. Then you can consider ways to manage the blows.

On occasions, you'll need to make reasonably speedy decisions to take advantage of an opportunity. You also need to 'look before you leap'. If faced with a challenge or chance that opposes your goal, it is valuable to stop, pause and think before acting (especially where the decisions involve a serious level of commitment). I've seen an unfortunate number of small businesses perceive something to be an opportunity they can't ignore, and grab it, only to find it has completely sent them on a course removed from their core purpose and goals.

Common generic goals for small businesses

The following are the most common goals you will come across for small businesses.

1. **I want to start a new business.**

2. **I want to maintain the business, but make it more profitable.**

3. **I want to buy an existing business.**

4. **I want to sell the business — in part or in full.**

5. **I want to grow the business.**

6. **I want to be less involved in the business — by choice or through circumstance.**

7. **I must close the business.**

Lets now look at each f these generic goals in more detail.

GOAL 1   I want to start a new business

Starting your own business, by taking an idea and bringing it to life, is probably one of the most rewarding experiences you can have in your business career. This includes bringing an idea to life and gaining the freedom that comes with starting your own business.

There are many reasons you may have decided to start your own business. It may be to pursue an idea where you see a need or to create a job when no full-time jobs are available (as occurs in tighter economic times). It may be from the desire to achieve the independence brought about by self-employment or because you believe you can do it much better than your current boss. Whatever the reason, it is great that you're considering it.

However, any start-up can take significant effort to become financially sustainable. Starting is easy. Making it last is not so easy. Far too many start-ups don't survive.

> **The Definition of a Start-up**
> *"A human institution designed to deliver a new product or service under conditions of extreme uncertainty."*
> — Eric Ries, *The Lean Start-Up*

One of the greatest challenges in any start-up is accessing funds to get the business off the ground and then to keep it going. This is not only to cover product or service development but for you to live off, especially if you have given up a secure income to pursue your dream.

Even a start-up that requires only a small amount of initial funds can still take many months to see sales. How long can you last without income? That first customer or sale is like winning the lottery. You could be many months waiting for the first dollar and then many more months to get a stable income.

We cover a range of ways your business can attract external funds in later chapters. Whatever source of funding you choose, you need to ensure you can cover your costs to start up the business, meet commitments to funders and keep food on the table. Otherwise, it could be a very short-lived business venture.

If you have established that you can satisfy these criteria, then we can get into the process of getting your business going and keeping it going.

Some successful start-up stories

Much of the literature you see on start-ups seems to apply to those IT ideas that go from nothing to multi-million/billion-dollar ventures. However, there is a wide range of start-ups that experience significant growth.

Here are a few examples that may or may not be well known to you. While they may not reflect what you are hoping to do, they are still very inspiring. Most show individuals achieving the success they sought, with limited business skills, chasing an idea without much money behind them but having a heap of passion.

- *Navman*

  Navman is the car and marine navigation business. It was started by (the now Sir) Peter Maire in his garage in 1986. The firm was sold to a North American conglomerate in 2004 for over $100 million.

- *RioLife*

  While travelling and surfing the world at just 23 years old, with little money, Jeremy Liddle, Andrew Cameron and Andrew Maciver discovered the berry called *açai* in Brazil. When they returned to Australia, they blended a product from the berries and started the company RioLife. It was voted Australia's fastest-growing small business in 2010. RioLife is now Australia's leading importer of *açai* berries.

- *GoPro*

  Nick Woodman formed GoPro cameras in 2002 after being frustrated that he could not get quality action photos at a surfing competition. Woodman initially raised money for his company by selling bead and shell belts out of his VW van. Each belt sold for under $US 20. On 26 June 2014, the company raised $US 427 million on its first day as a publicly traded company. At the price it was initially listed on the stock exchange, it would be worth $US 2.95 billion.

- *InStitchu*

  James Wakefield and Robin McGown met at University and started InStitchu while still in their corporate jobs. InStitchu is an online store for tailored suits. The company now has showrooms in Sydney, Melbourne and Brisbane, and are planning to enter the US next. It was valued (in 2017) at $10 million.

These are inspiring stories that I hope motivate you. If you looked at the mix of this small list, you might think that the only successful entrepreneurs are young geeks or hippies with not much money and huge drive.

The reality of start-up businesses is very different to this perception. The average start-up (based on UK statistics) is led by men in their forties with previous work experience. Women led only 12% of start-ups. I know of many women who are trying to start businesses and I truly hope this continues so these figures start to change.

The 'lean start-up' process

If your start-up involves a new product or unique service, and there isn't a lot of readily available information about how it will go, you may need to think a little more carefully about how to proceed. The product or service may need a reasonable level of cash and your time to get it ready for sale. You will then need to do a lot more to market the product than would be the case for a business with a well-known product or service.

What if you invest a heap of time and money only to find it doesn't sell? What if your great idea proves to be of modest interest to everyone else? How do you know what will and won't sell when the idea is relatively new?

Eric Ries, a 34-year-old Yale graduate and (yes, you guessed it) an entrepreneur, developed a concept to address this challenge. His book *The Lean Startup* took the traditional concept of 'lean manufacturing' and applied it to the process of start-ups. His desire to write the book came from the failure of one of his early companies, successes in later companies, as well as his time with start-up incubators and venture capitalists.

The traditional 'lean manufacturing' concept was born from Toyota's improvement processes in the 1930s. While lean defines a process to identify and then remove waste from the way a business is run, it is also a culture. While it can be applied to any business, even small businesses, it is more common in larger, more complex, process- and manufacturing-based industries.

Ries applied the 'lean' concept to start-ups in the following ways:

- Take smaller steps in your product or service development, testing and retesting the market as your product or service evolves.
- Take a 'minimum viable product' to some level of market release to gain feedback from customers before seeking perfection. This then allows you to revisit the product or service, fine-tune it and do a further validation.
- Fail often, fail cheaply, and avoid continuing on a path to disaster by powering on blindly. Eric Ries put this in terms of 'pivoting' (changing direction) or 'preserving' (continuing on the same path) based on the incremental feedback you receive.

Some practical realities of starting a business

There are many other less-than-sexy tasks you must do when starting up your business. While it's great to get wrapped up in the new product, at least put some of your energy into some housekeeping issues about your new business.

Will you have enough money to live off?

Unfortunately, many people setting out on the journey to start their small business very quickly come unstuck when they realise it won't make the money they expected early in its life. If is very common for start-up businesses to take many months, even years, before they make enough money to pay the owner a decent wage. People who give up a job that pays on a regular basis, and offers enough money to pay the bills, may get a shock when their start up does not deliver the same, at least initially.

When starting up your new business think very carefully, not only how you will fund the set-up of your new business, but how you will fund your day-to-day living expenses if the business doesn't bring the money in as quick as you had hoped. If you need the start up to make a certain amount of money very early in its life it will start putting immense pressure on you. You will feel pressured to pursue work and customers that are not in keeping with your values. You may find yourself discounting your pricing just to get work. You may find yourself working ridiculous hours and seriously impacting your health. This could cause irreparable damage to your brand, cause significant stress, and may see the dream of your start-up ending before it even gets a chance to succeed.

Here are some suggestions:

- Keep your full-time job and use your weekends, and holidays to set up the business.
- See if you can go part-time in your job or swap your full-time job for a part-time job.
- Seek some contract work while setting up your start-up.
- If you have a personal partner who is working (e.g. a wife or husband) see if you can live off one wage.
- Look seriously at your spending and see what you can cut back while starting the business.
- Consider what personal savings you can sacrifice to get the small business going.
- See if you can access other funding to cover the costs of your start-up and initial living costs — BUT be warned — read the chapters on seeking money from others so you understand the risk.

What company structure will best suit your new business?

After you test your ideas, you will need to turn your idea into a business and then run the business. You will need to decide what legal structure your business should have.

While there are many structures that exist in different countries, there are three principle structures that small businesses are likely to take on.

1. Sole Trader or Sole Proprietorship

A sole trader is a business started and run by one individual. There are usually no formal or legal processes required to set up a sole trader. Typically, this type of business can spring into existence when you decide to become your own boss; whether that's cutting lawns, building websites, cleaning homes or cutting people's hair. This is the most common of all company structures in OECD countries. In the 2012 census in the US, sole traders exceeded 20 million in number and in the UK they exceeded 3 million.

If this is you, welcome to a very large international business community. However, just because there are a lot of them does not necessarily mean it's the best choice for you. The owner of a sole trader is personally entitled to all profits, but is also personally liable for all business taxes. Effectively, you pay tax through your personal tax return.

The main advantages of a sole trader is that it is very easy to open, subject to relatively few regulations, fully autonomous with regard to the owner's business decisions, and easy to discontinue.

On the flip side, you are personally liable for any debt. That is, as the owner, your liability is unlimited. This is one of the major disadvantages of a sole trader. A sole trader can be held personally liable for any and all business-related debts and obligations. If your business defaults on a loan or fails to pay suppliers, for instance, those parties could legally pursue your personal possessions to get their money.

It may also be more messy trying to employ other people as a sole trader than other legal structures, as you grow. Sole traders are harder to fund or sell, if that becomes your goal, because people outside the business will see no distinction between you and the business. These risks for a sole trader are likely to increase as your business grows. While a sole trader may be the simplest place to start your business as a solo, you may need to consider changing that as you develop.

Sole traders can find they simply bought themselves a job rather than a business, if they don't adequately separate themselves from the business.

Therefore, if you intend starting your business, remaining a solo and not growing and are unlikely to take on debts, enter into supplier agreements or employ people than a sole trader may be all you need. However, you will need to look seriously at shifting to a more formal business structure if you have any intentions of growing.

2. Partnership

A partnership involves a contract between two or more people to engage in business. Assets and responsibilities are shared by the partnership. Like a sole trader, a partnership is not a separate legal entity.

Usually each partner contributes finances, property, skill or labour, although a party may contribute nothing and still have the rights of a partner. There can be different types of partnerships that may alter the level of their involvement, liabilities and tax.

As you enter a business relationship, you should consider the right legal documents to support the relationship. This does not indicate either party lacks trust in the other. It is simply good business practice. Businesses and people change. Things go wrong. You need to have professional documentation to reflect your views on the relationship.

Before discussing the legal and contractual aspects of the relationship, you need to discuss candidly the personal aspects of the partnership. Having a partner or partners for the wrong reasons (such as having capital or being a family member) could end in disaster. You both need to voice the issues you consider important before facing them.

What happens if one partner wants to leave? What happens if one partner believes the other is not pulling their weight? How do you manage a dispute over the future direction of the business?

Have the debate before you start, not when you hit your first business speed bump. These discussions may be far more effective if you use an independent third party experienced in partnerships. They will be able to pose questions to you and your partner(s) that you may not consider or are simply reluctant to address.

These discussions can be even more difficult if the partners are in a personal relationship, like a husband and wife, friends or family. It is important to discuss the possible worst-case scenarios and how you will manage disputes when everyone is in the right frame of mind (at the start of the relationship or when everything is going well). Look at the business as a separate entity to the personal relationship.

It is really important to get a well-documented partnership agreement prepared by a lawyer experienced in this type of commercial work.

3. Limited Liability Company (LLC).

There are a number of more formal legal entities a business could choose that separate themselves for the business. The most common is a Limited Liability Company (LLC). New Zealand is one of the easiest places on the planet to set up a company, as detailed in the World Banks survey on the ease of doing business in various countries.

The key considerations in setting up a company rather than a sole trader or partnership include:

- A company is a legal entity in itself and is considered to be completely separate to you. Many non-employer or solo businesses set up a company to create this separation. This will force discipline because you will normally produce a set of accounts that provides a clear separation between the business activities and private activities.
- The liabilities faced by the owner of a company are likely to be very different to those of a sole trader. The term Limited Liability Company is a very important consideration. If the business gets into trouble, it will be critical to understand what exposure the business has to losses and what personal liability you have for them.

Limited liability means that there is a wall between your personal assets and your business assets. For example, a supplier is unlikely to get access to your assets if your LLC gets into trouble. The LLC can lose everything it owns. However, it cannot result in the loss of the assets of its owners (or shareholders). Limited liability doesn't refer to the amount at risk. It refers to a separation between business and personal assets.

An important word of caution. Many lenders such as banks and some creditors may only lend you money or supply you goods and services if you give them a personal guarantee that the funds will be repaid. For many small businesses, you may have little choice until you build up a track record and cash within your business. The personal guarantee may be backed by private assets. In this case, the lender may become a secured creditor and your liability will include the business and those assets you put up as security. Ensure you are clear what you could lose if the business fails. It does not mean you should avoid this strategy. All it means is you are entering it with your eyes wide open. Please do your homework and seek advice on these issues. This is not an area you ever want to get into without fully understanding it.

Taxation also differs for a LLC. Taxation will vary depending on what form your business takes and what the tax laws are in your country, state or region. This is where you need to call on the experts, as tax is a major driver in the type of business structure you could choose.

> 👉 *The key point to remember about taxation when setting up and running your business is that tax has a major impact. However, don't let the tail wag the dog. First and foremost, make good business decisions and **after that** make good tax decisions.*

Consider what legal documents you might need. If you have other parties that will be shareholders with you, it's important to develop a shareholders agreement. The same uncertainties that were mentioned for a partnership will apply here. How will you handle a situation where one shareholder wants to sell their shares? What happens if you want to bring additional shareholders into the business? How do you value the business in these situations? What happens if one party wants to take a very different direction in the business to another party? That might be a business sale or growth strategy. Who has what decision-making powers?

The key considerations to keep in mind when deciding on which structure to choose include:

- The cost to set up each option
- The tax implications on the business and on you depending on the choice
- The level of liability you will face personally if the business gets into trouble
- The ease of administering one business structure over another
- Separating you from the business.
- Your longer-term plans — stay small or grow.

Once you feel you have gained some level of understanding of the options and an understanding of the key differences, it is then time to seek advice.

Systems and processes

If you are starting a small business, whether Sole Trader, Partnership or Limited Liability Company, you will need to set up some workable systems from day one, particularly to help manage your money. The sophistication of the systems you choose will depend as much on your budget as anything. We will get into some deeper discussion on systems and processes in later chapters.

For now, just accept you are going to need them and plan to do something about them.

GOAL 2   I want to maintain the business, but make it more profitable

Many small businesses feel some pressure to grow to demonstrate that they have achieved business success. However, many of small business owners do not want to pursue significant growth. Many owners have chosen a business with limited growth potential. They may also be at a point in their lives where they simply don't want the added stress that comes with significant growth.

However, I am yet to come across a small business that doesn't want to improve their profitability and free up their time to pursue other things.

In choosing this as your goal, you have not precluded the opportunity to pursue growth later. Getting your business in strong shape and putting additional cash in the bank allows you to choose other goals, including growth.

☞ *If you would love to grow and believe your business has genuine opportunities to do so, I hope you haven't chosen this goal simply because of a fear of failure or taking risks. If you're looking at this goal solely because of these fears, be brave and jump ahead to the goal of growth, before settling on this path.*

To build a stronger, more profitable business requires you to look at all aspects of your business, as we will cover in this book. A strong set of values, a clear purpose and a distinct point of difference. From here, it requires appropriate sales and marketing, management of your staff (if you have any), good systems and a strong understanding of your finances.

Therefore, there is no one answer to the question of profitability.

A few simple tips to become more profitable

I will briefly jump ahead and consider some of the concepts around profitability, which we'll cover in more detail when we dig into your business's finances. These tips are just to whet your appetite on how to start improving profitability.

'Profit' and 'profitability' are concepts that we all feel we know. However, they can be misunderstood. People often use the terms profit and revenue interchangeably, but they mean very different things. Add to these other terms, such as 'net profit after tax', 'profit before tax', 'gross margin' and things can get a little confusing. Here are a few helpful tips on what these terms mean:

- The money coming into the business from the sale of your product and/or services is your **revenue**. The more you sell, the more revenue you make.
- To produce and sell goods and/or services, each sale will require the use of raw materials and labour. These are termed your **cost of sales**. These costs are variable. This means they drop when the revenue drops, and they increase when revenue increases. If sales stopped and revenue stopped, your cost of sales should also go to zero.

- The next part of the story is your **overheads** or your **expenses**. You must meet these expenses whether you are selling or not. These are fixed costs.
- When I say **profit**, I mean what's left over after you take all your costs of sales and expenses.

After this, the banks will take interest on any borrowings. You will also account for the deterioration in the value of your assets with depreciation, a discussion we'll leave until later. Finally, the taxman takes his cut. After all this, you are left with your net profit after tax.

Revenue
– Cost of Sales
_____
= Gross Margin
– Expenses
_____
= Earnings
– Interest
– Depreciation
– Taxation
_____
= Net Profit after Tax

Where does the cash go in your small business?

Let's show how the cash that comes into your business flows out of the business to see what ends up in the business's bank account. Remember, this is the business's bank account, not the owner's bank account.

Cash flows into the business from sales. After all the cash associated with costs are removed the business is left with its profit (excluding depreciation which is not cash). The cash that is left over becomes the Retained Earnings that will appear in the Balance Sheet. There will also be a range of different amounts of cash coming into and out of the business, which will appear in the balance sheet.

The profit needs to fund the repayment of any loans the business may have. It may have to fund the purchase of new equipment. It may also be used to pay the owner of the business as drawings or dividends.

After all this, the hope is there is some cash left in the business's bank account.

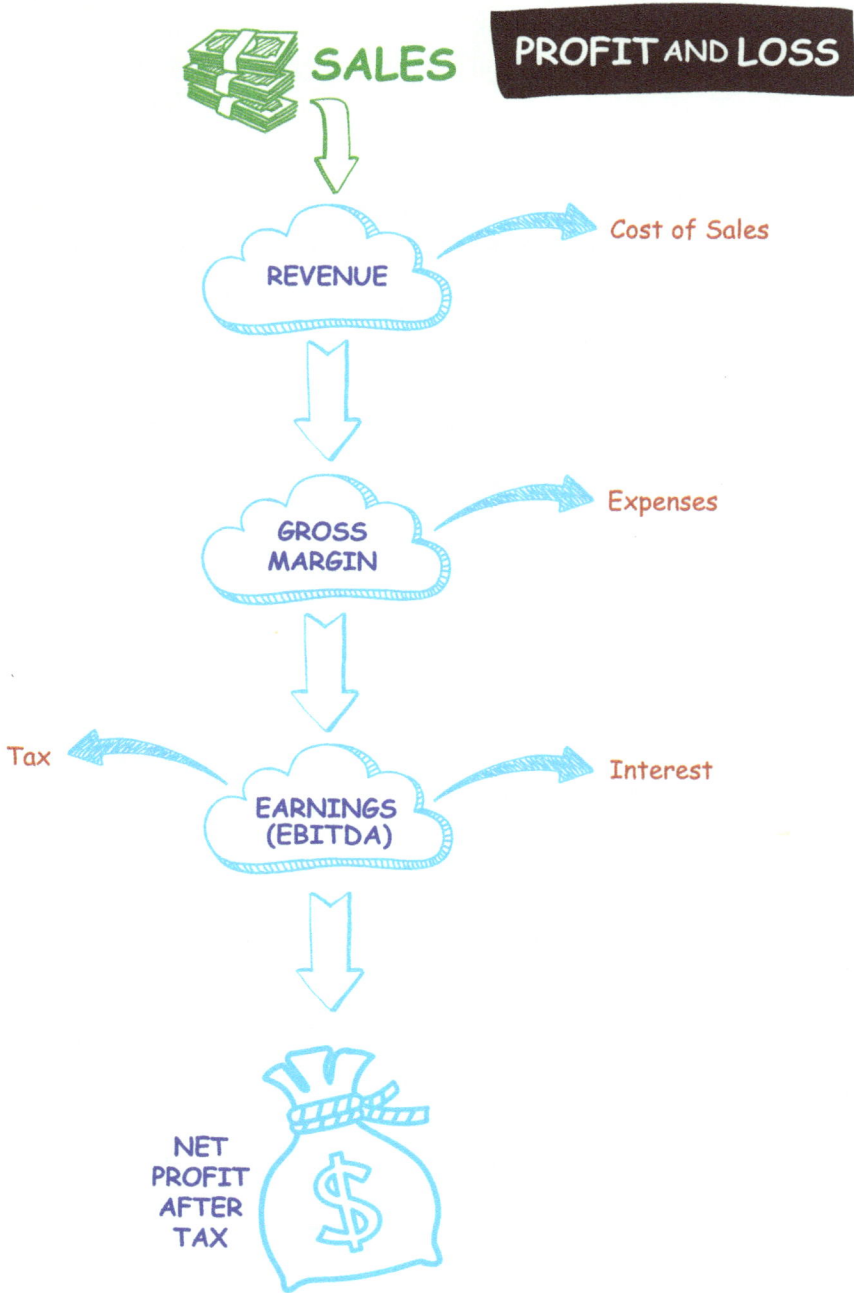

SALES

PROFIT AND LOSS

REVENUE

Cost of Sales

GROSS MARGIN

Expenses

EARNINGS (EBITDA)

Tax

Interest

NET PROFIT AFTER TAX

Fig. 4a: Where did the cash go? Year 1

RETAINED EARNINGS (NET PROFIT AFTER TAX, from previous years)

BALANCE SHEET

Cash from previous years

Funds introduced (You or bank)

CASH FROM YOUR OPERATIONS

Payments to owner (You)

Loan repayments

Purchase new assets

BANK

WHAT'S LEFT!

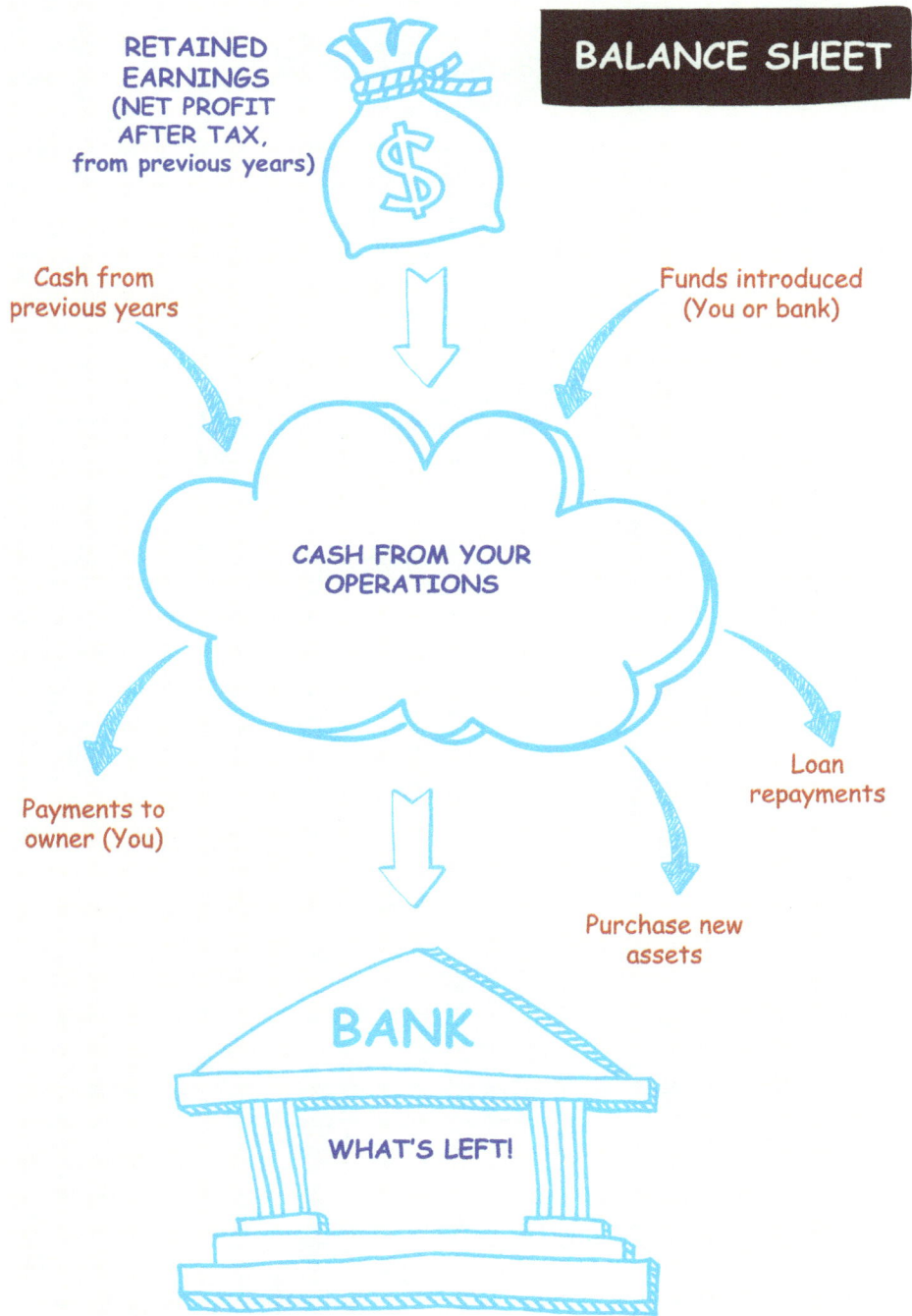

Fig. 4b: Where did the cash go? Year 1

I will go through this in much greater detail in Chapter 12..

Is there a silver bullet to achieve profitability?
Your business will become more **profitable** by:

- increasing your sales and the revenue you make from those sales
- reducing the cost of each sale, or
- lowering your fixed costs, tax or interest without impacting your ability to sell.

This applies to every business no matter what size. It sounds pretty straightforward but, as I'm sure you know, it's not that simple. The strategy you set and your frame of mind will play a big part in achieving this. You will now need to read further on in the book to see how you should plan, how to market your products, manage your staff, manage your cash flow, manage your funding and finances, and all aspects of your day-to-day operations. All these will play some part in achieving greater profitability.

The Lone Ranger, first appearing on a 1933 radio show, used silver bullets to bring an instant solution, and justice, to a problem. I'm sorry but it's very rare to find silver bullets in small business.

GOAL 3   I want to buy an existing business

Buying an existing business may be a far more appealing option than a start-up. An existing business will have an existing market, customers, property, plant and equipment, inventory and possibly a few employees. It will also, hopefully, start earning you an income from the day you buy it.

The challenge will be choosing the right business, knowing what you are getting, raising the money to buy the business and then being able to run the business once you have purchased it. Like anything, you will get what you pay for.

There are many stories of buyers finding quite a different business when they come to run it compared with what was offered to them. The other major issue is if the buyer gets emotionally attached to a business and fails to see the full picture before completing the purchase.

1. Choose the right business for you
Before buying a business, you must be clear on the following questions:

- Why are you buying the business? Employment? Independence? Income? Lifestyle?
- What is your long-term goal following the purchase?
- What do you enjoy doing?
- What are you good and bad at that will impact on your decision?

You should be cautious buying into a business where you have limited skills. This is not a time for your emotions to drive your decision. While you need to be passionate about it, if you look at the purchase through rose-coloured glasses, you could be left with significant regret. If you feel you are not being objective enough, call on some independent eyes.

2. This is not a process to do alone

You need to set aside some funds to find, review and then purchase the business. No matter how simple or small the business you are buying, you will still need to call on external expertise. Typically, you should consider using the following experts:

- **A business broker or business sales expert**. They can find the business for you and carry out a far more accurate valuation than you can. When you choose these people, do your homework. The good ones will be happy to share their success rates, i.e. what is the percentage of businesses have they taken on and valued and how many have they sold? This will highlight how accurate their valuations were.
- **An accountant**. This is to ensure you've considered tax issues and to review all the financial reports. You also want to ensure you get an accurate and complete set of financial accounts, not a set that the seller wants you to see. A good accountant will see this. Some accountants will also be able to do a valuation of the business. Just be careful. This is a specialised area and those doing it need to be doing it often. Many accountants perform this service rarely.
- **A lawyer.** This is to prepare and/or review all legal issues existing with the business and any agreements related to the purchase. You may also need assistance in setting up your own company structure for the purchase.
- **Specific technical experts**. They can assist in reviewing the business if it has aspects that are unique to that industry.

Even if you are buying a small business with limited capital outlay, you want to get it right. So you need to think through who can best assist you.

3. Agreements

The seller is very likely to require you to sign a confidentiality agreement before they allow you any access to their business. This will protect the seller from you handing this information to others, especially if you choose not to proceed with the sale.

Some sellers may be looking to sell confidentially and are not keen to make it known to competitors or employees. It is likely this will be covered in the confidentiality agreement. While this may limit how widely or openly you discuss the sale, you still should be comfortable that you're able to assess everything about the business that you need to make a decision.

You and the seller may also decide to sign a conditional sale and purchase agreement at the start of the process. This will likely include confidentiality clauses and what you, as the buyer, need to investigate. It may also indicate conditions under which you may be allowed to withdraw from the process.

4. How much can you afford?

As with any purchase, you will get what you pay for. It's essential that you're very clear on what you can afford though too. It is possible you will have to seek external funds to buy the business. The greater the amount of external funding you require, the greater will be the pressure on you to buy a business that will deliver the cash to pay off these funds. If you are required to access these external funds by securing them against personal assets, this will add pressure. For example, if it all fails, you may lose your house.

> *"If you can't afford it, you can't afford it."*
> — **My grandmother**

5. *Caveat Emptor* — Buyer Beware

You need to heed this long-standing legal term before buying.

The technical term for the process of investigating the business is **due diligence** or, more simply, look as carefully as you can at the business to ensure you know what you're buying. Write down a due diligence checklist and make the owner very clear about your expectations before the process begins. You should do some general searching in the marketplace, online and in the media to gain as much knowledge as you can.

- How are other similar businesses being priced for sale?
- Are you able to establish the brand exposure and reputation of the business?
- What are the perceptions of their brand?
- Are there any discussions or reports on the business on mainstream or social media?

The more detail you can find on the business, the more confident you can be in the price you negotiate. Here are a few things you should consider at as part of the due diligence:

- Request a full set of professionally produced annual financial accounts. At least the last three years. Don't accept edited or abridged accounts.
- Assess what the owners are paying themselves and if it is consistent with market rates (the way owners include their salary can have a big impact on the value of the business, a good broker will know how to factor this into the valuation).
- Assess if there are any costs that do not reflect market rates that will impact you after the sale (e.g. the owners don't pay rent on a family-owned property, but you will have to).
- Assess how reliant the business is on the owner.
- Review the systems being used to run the business.
- Assess the state of any assets that the business relies on (debts should not be your concern, but remain with the owner).
- Determine what debts are tied to the business.

- Access and read all legal documents, contracts and agreements.
- Establish if there are any outstanding legal matters relating to the business. Seek legal advice.
- Do as much market research as you can to establish if past revenue will reflect potential future revenue.
- Get the details of all staff members who will stay with the business.

Buying a Franchise

What is a franchise?

Franchising is the practice where an established business (the franchisor) sells another person (the franchisee) the right to trade using their trademarks, systems, processes and experience. This is a widely successful business model operated by McDonald's, Subway, Hertz, Century 21, Baskin Robbins, Cartridge World and thousands more.

The franchisee must operate the business in accordance with the franchisor's requirements (typically covered in a franchise agreement). The franchisee must pay fees to the franchisor. The agreement will define what the franchisor will provide to the franchisee in the way of systems, processes, training and support.

If you're buying a franchise, the core principles of doing so are no different to buying any business. You need to consider the same issues. There are, however, some clear advantages to choosing a franchise, especially if it's your first business.

These advantages include:
- Entry into a business with an existing and well-recognised brand
- Processes and systems that have been proven over time
- Training and support
- A more detailed record of past performance across a number of businesses
- An immediate network of other franchisees to refer to for help
- The legal right to use an existing brand and systems
- Purchasing power where the franchisor purchases on behalf of all franchisees.

With these advantages will come restrictions that wouldn't apply in your own non-franchised business. You won't have total control. You have to work with the restrictions the franchisor lays down: what you can sell, how you sell, when you sell it, ingredients you use, equipment you buy, and so on. You may have to contribute to marketing campaigns. If you have innovative ideas to market or grow your franchise, you may be restricted in what you can do under the terms of the franchise agreement.

Before you commit to the purchase, you need to check if the franchisor will deliver what it says it will offer, including systems and processes, training and marketing. Some franchisors may over-promise and then, after you buy, under-deliver. One of the best ways to establish this is to contact other franchisees in the same business.

Avoid the temptation to ignore the franchisor's requirements and do your own thing. If the systems are proven, there is good reason to follow them. If they don't meet your needs, discuss them with the franchisor before you unilaterally change them. As you are likely to be in this relationship for many years, you need to know as much as you can about the franchise owners. You want to know about their experience in franchising and business in general.

☞ *You should not get a false sense of security that franchising is easy. Just because other businesses in the same franchise have been successful does not mean you will be successful. You have to work just as hard, follow the same core business principles as any other business model.*

Franchise agreement

This is a critical document that you need to read and understand. There is benefit in referring it to your legal advisor if there are any parts of the agreement you don't fully comprehend.

These agreements will vary from franchise to franchise, but will include factors such as:

- The initial investment required
- All franchise fees (upfront and ongoing)
- Penalties for breaching requirements of the agreement (e.g. late payment charges, trademark breaches)
- Duration of the agreement
- Any geographical limitations on where you can sell
- Obligations on and performance expectations for you
- Obligations on and performance expectations of the franchisor
- Stock to be included
- The products and services you can and can't sell
- Premises, leases and other equipment to be included
- Your legal rights over intellectual property use (logos, trademarks, copyrights, patents)
- Process for the sale of the franchise
- Termination, defining how either party can bring the franchise relationship to an end
- Restraint of trade, defining what you can and can't do when you are operating the franchise and also after you leave (periods where you can't open a directly competing business or employ people from the franchise)
- Dispute resolution procedures.

It is unlikely you will have a lot of scope to alter the agreement, especially with mature or long-standing franchises. This emphasises the need to fully understand the document so you know exactly what you are getting yourself into.

Franchise fees

All franchises will have to pay fees to the franchisor. The amount and form these fees take will vary from franchise to franchise. Ensure you're fully aware of all fees and to assess whether you believe they are good value for money. The key is less about the amount of fees but more about what value they bring to your business. It is not uncommon for a franchisor to promise a high level of support at the time of purchase, but you find a very different reality once you are in the business. Fees typically involve an initial investment and then ongoing fees. The following are typical of what you will find in widely known international franchises. Smaller franchises are likely to bundle these into simpler fee structures.

Initial investment costs could include:

- Initial franchise fee
- Property
- Furniture, fixtures and equipment
- Exterior signage
- Opening inventory
- Insurance
- Training expenses
- Legal and accounting
- Opening advertising.

Ongoing fees could include:

- Royalty either as a percentage of sales (typically 4–10% of sales) and/or a fixed fee
- Advertising fees
- Equipment lease fees
- Property lease fees
- Insurance costs
- Fee for use of systems.

How to negotiate the final deal

Many people view the skill of negotiation as a gift: that some people have it and some don't. This is not the case. Negotiation is a process. If you enter a negotiation prepared and follow some key principles, you will be as well placed to negotiate a favourable outcome as anyone. I will summarise a few of these principles, as they apply to buying a business:

- **Be prepared!**
  Do all your homework on the business before negotiating a price. This includes all the points mentioned above.
- **Understand the seller.**
  Do as much as you can to understand the motives and needs of the seller. This is just as important as knowing your own needs and motives.
- **Know your 'BATNA'.**
  There is a term used in negotiation called BATNA, which means the 'Best Alternative

To a Negotiated Agreement'. It defines the course of action you will take if the negotiations fail and an agreement cannot be reached. As a buyer, you may simply walk away and move on to another option. However, if you are not clear where this point is, you may walk away prematurely and miss out on a great deal or you could get emotionally attached and continue when you should have walked away. You should also consider what the seller's BATNA is likely to be.

- **Be the first to offer a price.**

  If the seller has not quoted a price, be the first to state what you want to pay before the seller states their price. This is the point from which all subsequent discussions will be taken. There is science behind this. It is called **anchoring**, or in psychological terms, it creates a **cognitive bias**. (If you're interested in the details behind this, have a look at the work of Nobel laureate Daniel Kahneman, starting back in 1974.) Basically, by pricing first, you dictate the starting point for the negotiation. Be cautious not to offer a ridiculous price. The seller may laugh and walk away. Offer the lowest price you think you can while keeping the seller interested. If the seller has already listed a price, you need to be cautious about being trapped in your own cognitive bias based on this price. If you have done your homework, you should know if the price has any merit.

- **Be careful about time pressures.**

  Almost all concessions in a negotiation are made in the last stages of a negotiation. The person under the greatest time pressure is likely to make the most concessions. Always be cautious about drifting outside your parameters just because a date has been set.

GOAL 4   I want to sell the business — in part or in full

There are many reasons why you may want to sell your business. In fact, it is likely that any business that survives for long enough will go through some form of sale process. Some are sold for the right reasons but some aren't. Here's how to determine good reasons for selling.

Be cautious about selling just because you want out

I have advised and supported business owners that have emotionally 'hit a wall'. They have been through very tough times, lost interest and desire to go on in the business, and simply want out. This is not a good mindset or time from which to be considering a sale. Instead, it's an important moment to seek a calm external voice. A sale may not be a good option as it could potentially leave you in a worse situation emotionally and financially (for example, where the business is worth little but leaves you with significant debt).

Assuming this is not the situation for you, we will now go through some key considerations in selling your business.

Why some businesses just don't sell

The reality is that many small businesses go on the market and simply don't sell, at least the first time.

There is a range of reasons for this:

- Past profitability is not great.
- The future for the business or the industry sector is not strong.
- The business is overvalued (so the owner expects too much).
- The business is too risky.
- The owner is the business. If he or she leaves, there is no business.
- There is a lack of good systems or processes.
- No-one is willing to lend money to buyers on the basis of the business.
- There is a lack of interested buyers.
- The business is not packaged or marketed properly.
- There may be messy legal, property or security issues attached to aspects of the business.

How do you make your small business 'sellable'?

The first critical question if you are a small business is whether you have a business that can be sold.

Make it more profitable

Business buyers looking to buy your business as a going concern are primarily looking for cash flow, good systems, and a business with a future. So prepare by reducing unnecessary expenses and increasing sales to improve cash flow.

If your business has strong potential but you have failed to realise that potential in terms of profitability, then you may well get an interested buyer who will buy your business for a lower price and then, through their actions, produce the cash flow you were unable to produce.

If you genuinely believe you have much greater potential to increase profits but are struggling to realise it, then it may be time to round up some expertise to see what you are missing. If you are able to realise this profitability, you may be less inclined to sell, but if you do still want to sell, then you should attract a much better price.

Make it transferable

It has to survive without you. How *transferable* is the business?

If you are the business, and you leave, then no-one is likely to want to buy it. Before considering the process of selling your business, you need to discuss how to turn your small business into something worth selling. This is something that could take a number of years to achieve. This is why strategies like a business sale need to be considered well ahead of time.

If you explore the different methods of valuing a business outlined in Chapter 14, you will see that the factors contributing to increased value of your business and the factors making it appealing to a buyer are the same. And they are the exact same improvements that will make your business successful for you even if you wanted to keep it.

The best way to make the business more independent of you is to start bringing in additional people (if you have no internal capacity) and start delegating activities to them. The more developed your systems and processes, the better the chance for another person to pick up and run the business without you being there. If everything is in your head, it may be time to start writing it down and loading it into a suitable system.

This also applies to the goal of handing over the operations of the business to someone else. By setting yourself up for this handover, it leaves you with the choice of taking a less operational role in the business or selling it.

Make your offerings more unique

If your small business is selling products that are in demand, especially if they are unique, the value of your business will be higher. Depending on your role, it is also more likely the business will operate independently of you because the value is in the product and not you.

If you are simply selling products that are the same as everyone else, you will need to really work on your point of difference.

Service 'productisation'

If you run a service-based business where you provide the service, the business is likely to have limited ability to grow because it is limited by the hours you can work. It may well be very profitable. However, if the services cannot be offered by anyone else in the business then its value is likely to be zero.

If you are able to turn these services into standardised products that are more easily replicated, then other people can deliver them to a standard similar to you. You could also sell or license the use of the products to other businesses.

Your challenge may be to ensure you are still able to offer your customers a unique service, but with increased repeatability.

An example of service productisation at Wordy.com

Let's look at an example of an online business that turned what is typically a service offering into a product. The business is called Wordy.com.

Typically, if you want to get some of your text edited (like a university thesis, book or other document), you approach an editor who offers this service. This could be a solo businessperson, one of many you could have approached, who goes through your text and sends it back edited. Wordy.com is an online editing business started by Anders Schepelern, an editor and businessperson who has started up a number of small businesses. He has turned text editing into a business that now offers standardised editing services, involving four price packages, with standard delivery times.

There are a number of in-house and freelance editors behind the scenes to edit your documents to a standard. Wordy.com sets this standard, then trains and verifies editors to meet it. The service does not rely on a single person, because there are many editors that you should have confidence will meet your needs.

This is clearly a business model that could be valued and, while it is unclear what it is worth, there is no doubt it has significantly greater value than if Anders Schepelern was doing the editing on his own.

Does increasing the value of your assets increase the value of the business?

The correct answer to this question is maybe. If you increase the physical assets in your business, some valuation techniques may indicate that this has increased the value of the business. However, the example below indicates why you need to be cautious.

Say you decided to buy the building you currently rent, in the hope that it will strengthen your balance sheet (with more assets). This purchase is unlikely to increase your sales in any way. It may bring with it debt. If the buyer is indifferent whether to buy or rent the property, and wants your business unencumbered from debt, then this asset could actually turn them away.

Intellectual property (IP) can also add value, if a potential buyer sees that it will bring future profitability. Intellectual property includes:

- Patents
- Trademarks
- Internet domain names
- Customer lists
- Customer loyalty
- The reputation of the business
- The skills of the employees
- Contracts for future work
- Order backlog
- Licensing agreements
- Franchise agreements
- Employment contracts
- Trade secrets (e.g. secret formulas or recipes).

I will discuss the details of how to protect and grow your intellectual property in Chapter 10.

If you have developed real value in your brand, your reputation, systems and processes, staff competencies, patents and trademarks (collectively called **goodwill**), then it is likely to add value to the selling price of your business. However, be cautious here. This IP is only worth something if it will ultimately lead to more cash coming into the business.

You may see an item in your financial accounts labelled as 'goodwill'. Treat this with prudence, too. A buyer is unlikely to give any credence to this value when deliberating. It is really only an accounting term, not a market value.

Part-sale or shared ownership

You may wish to sell only a part of your business and are looking for someone outside to buy into it. This will be a more difficult task for a small business than a larger business. Interest may come if your small business shows potential for significant growth. People who are already close to you (family, friends, employees, or a close colleague) may express interest for reasons other than growth.

The reasons a part-sale might be appealing for you are:

- To provide additional funds that you would otherwise not have access to
- To bring different skills to the business
- To increase the long-term commitment a person will have for the business if they are a part-owner
- To retain critical staff by giving them a level of ownership
- To assist in sharing the workload and risk.

You do, however, need to be very mindful of the risks:

- With joint ownership comes joint decision-making and control. What if you can't agree?
- If there is an existing personal relationship with the potential partner then it may change. It may put undue pressure on that relationship (e.g. family members or friends taking ownership).
- The excitement of getting another person involved can soon sour when you get to know each other in the stressful environment of business ownership. This is particularly the case if your values are not aligned.
- It can be more difficult for an owner to get out of the business because the remaining party can't afford to buy them out.
- If you want to sell the business at a later date, the new owner could block the sale.
- If the part-sale involves ownership for an employee, it can get very difficult if the employee's performance drops and requires disciplinary action.

A critical consideration before proceeding with a shared ownership arrangement is a detailed shareholder's agreement. This needs to consider a wide range of scenarios, good or bad, that may arise in the future. It is much better to reach an impasse before the part-sale goes ahead than after it is complete.

Put your business on the market

You have done all your homework and you are now keen to put the business on the market to see if you can attract interested parties.

At this advanced stage, you should have the key people to support you through the process. It is likely to be your accountant, business broker and/or lawyer. They will guide you on the key steps you will need to follow.

You should make some assessment of your likely buyers. What might they be looking for in a business and how should you present and pitch your business for sale? If you were selling your house, you would tidy it up and present it in the right light. It is no different with your business. You want to give buyers confidence in you and the business.

Formalise all your business systems and processes to allow the easiest transfer with the sale. Get all your financials in order and checked by an accountant. Ensure these are a complete set of tax-ready accounts. Giving the buyer abbreviated accounts won't build much confidence and may be seen as you trying to hide something.

You need to consider how public you want to make the sale. You may want to keep it as confidential as possible before going public. This may allow you to keep your intentions away from competitors and you may have a few staff members who you fear might leave because they are worried about losing their jobs.

Expect the buyer to do due diligence on the business and on you. They will want to have a really detailed look at everything. Assume potential buyers are astute and will find any skeletons. Trying to hide something is likely to backfire on you.

If you want to keep the process quiet and to protect your business, especially if they decide not to buy, ensure they have signed a confidentiality agreement and that they return all information to you at the end of the process. Professional business brokers are particularly good at putting the correct processes in place to sell your business. They can also confidentially market the business, vet only suitable buyers and leave you to run the business. A sale process can be very distracting and can take much longer than you think to finalise.

Restraints of trade

What might be the restrictions on your activities after the sale? Well, don't be surprised if the buyer requests some form of restriction on what you can do as part of the sale, such as staying on for a period of time or ensuring you don't steal customers when you go, take staff with you or set up in direct opposition. The buyer may request that these restrictions stay in place for six to twelve months or even longer depending on what you negotiate. All these points will typically form part of the sale and purchase agreement that needs to be negotiated.

As such, if you want to sell, have a think about what you are going to do next. You may not have complete freedom for a period of time.

Sale and purchase agreement

This is the key legal document that will cover all matters around the sale of the business. It could be signed as part of the due diligence process to set the expectations of both parties. It will typically include:

- What is and isn't included in the sale (e.g. lists of assets and equipment)
- Whether any of the assets included in the sale are tied to money owed to third parties
- Details of employees
- Restraint of trade, preventing the seller from competing with you after the sale
- Risks and insurance

- Inventory levels at handover
- Things the seller will want done before sale
- Confidentiality
- If signed pre-sale, conditions that may allow the seller to withdraw.

It is strongly advised that you seek expert legal advice before signing this agreement.

How to negotiate the final sale

If you have jumped over the section on buying a business, go back and read How to Negotiate the Final Deal. Whether buying or selling, having a strategy to negotiate will increase your chances of getting the best deal.

GOAL 5 I want to grow the business

One of the great opportunities about starting small in business is your ability to grow it. When I talk about growth here, I don't mean a steady increase in the profit in the business through improvements in efficiencies. I mean it in the context of developing new products, new locations, bigger market share or orders of magnitude increases in sales. While I fully understand it is not for everyone, I certainly love to see smal buinesses growing into a mid to large business, and beyond.

Growth, like any business venture, needs to be thought through. Uncontrolled growth can be just as dangerous as a major decline in your business. Both can end in tears. The risk is that you overcommit and fail to consider the worst-case scenarios.

Your small business may not set out to grow when you start but in many cases you may notice that your customers have the same passion for your product or service as you do. You start to see greater potential and now want to realise this. This is really exciting, but it can also be really scary.

Critical questions to ask yourself are:

- Do I want this growth?
- Does it fit with my goals?
- Does it align with my core purpose?
- Can I achieve it without compromising my core values?

Understandably, you may be saying, "Why wouldn't I go for it?" This is certainly what I would hope you say, but again success is what you define it to be. Your goals in starting the business may not have included the stress and workload that significant growth can bring. If it doesn't meet your goals, values and purpose, don't feel like you have to grow just because you can. If you decide it is what you want to pursue, then we will now discuss the things you need to consider.

Funding

You are unlikely to grow at any significant rate without access to external funding. The funding I will discuss is what is needed to take you from being a small business into a business that goes well beyond this.

As a start-up or solo, you may have been able to survive with an initial injection of your own savings and are now relying on internally generated cash (from sales) to continue operating. You may also have a small overdraft.

More substantial growth may require funding options well beyond this. If you can't access these funds, the growth could put significant pressure on you and your business. You may be unable to match sales to the rising costs of growth.

These funds can be in the form of debt (borrowings) or funds could come from equity (where someone injects money and takes part ownership of your business).

I cover all your funding options in Chapter 13. You will need to work your way through these carefully and fully understand the risks and advantages of the different options.

Staffing

If you are going to grow rapidly, you cannot do it alone. You will need more people involved. While you may be able to achieve growth using external parties, it is likely you will need to take on more full-time people within your business. As a solo, you may have always dreaded this prospect. This is something you need to think through, especially if managing staff is something you have been avoiding. However, if you get the right people and look after them, it could add significant value to the business and also allow you access to fresh new ideas.

Your role

Your role will also need to change. As you grow, you simply can't do everything like you may have done to date. You will need to become much more disciplined on what role you have to play in the growth process and what you can delegate.

Market validation

If your plan to grow involves new products and services in new markets, you will need to consider validating the market. This could involve getting products or services into the market at the lowest cost you can, but not at the expense of quality, to see what interest exists. Working like this will allow you to modify the products or services as your business grows. These are the same principles you would apply if you were starting a business.

Growth through joining or working with other businesses

You could certainly look to other like-minded businesses that you might be prepared to align with to grow through the shared capabilities of both businesses. This could be done informally or there are some more formal arrangements you could consider. As with any coming-together of partners, shareholders or companies, the success will depend heavily on an alignment of the parties, especially the clarity of purpose, core values and goals.

This could be achieved through:

- Two businesses agreeing to merge into one bigger business
- Buying an existing business and merging it into your existing business
- Two or more businesses joining together in a joint venture for a specific project
- Agreeing to work together through a formal or informal alliance or contractual relationship.

Growth plan

During a period of growth, you could feel like you are slightly out of control, managing continual change. While planning may seem like a lost cause due to the pace of the change, there is still a need to put plans in place, no matter how often you need to review them.

> *"In preparing for battle, I have always found that plans are useless, but planning is indispensable."*
> — **Dwight D. Eisenhower, former US General and President**

This plan needs to be very clear on reminding you of your purpose, your values, what you will and won't do, and your goals. You will need to plan ahead on when you may need additional funds, staff, or inventory. The timing of actions like these could make or break your growth. The planning process may also help you develop the discipline to stop before making decisions that you may have otherwise made on the run and later regret.

Some examples of what could happen if your planning slips:

1. If you foresee significant growth in sales, you may choose to invest in staff, stock and office space to match this growth. If sales do not meet expectations, you would be faced with significant fixed costs without the associated revenue.
2. If you commit to a significant increase in sales and offer a level of product and service quality, you could fail to deliver. Through a combination of not wanting to commit too many resources and sales outstripping your initial expectations, you wouldn't meet the quality or quantity to which you've committed. Customers would be very dissatisfied and your brand suffers irreparable damage.

Scenario planning

Scenario planning, like strategy, had its birth in the military. It is a technique that considers the history and past trends leading to the current situation. Rather than predicting a single future, it assumes that all predictions of the future are, to some extent, wrong. Instead of one view of the future, it considers a number of credible future scenarios. This will typically include a best and worst case, and a most likely scenario based on what you know now. The best- and worst-case scenarios are where you need to force yourself to consider the things that could go very well or really badly, and what you might do if that happens.

Remember Michelle? She can see real growth potential and wants to use some scenario planning to test possible futures.

Michelle's Growth Plan

The interest in Michelle's products has exceeded her expectations. Based on some simple market research, she believes she could easily increase her modest first-year sales over the next couple of years. Michelle believes she will need to borrow money (as the bank supports her view), employ a person, move out of her home and into a small office complex and purchase inventory. However, before proceeding she completes a very simple scenario planning process by creating three stories that reflect three possible futures:

1. The **"My Best Bet"** scenario (most likely). This is the one Michelle is planning to pursue. If growth matches this trend, the resources and funding will deliver this success.
2. The **"Oh No"** scenario (worst case). In this scenario, for any number of reasons, sales fall well below expectations.
3. The **"Champagne on Ice"** scenario (best case). In this scenario, for any number of reasons, sales expand well beyond expectations.

Michelle considered the consequences on the business and on her if the "Oh No" scenario occurred. She could be faced with more staff, debt, and new premises, but no sales to pay for them. She could put her own home at risk, as she has to use it as security to get a bank loan. However, she believes if this did occur she could lay off staff (even though she would hate doing this) because she has options in their contracts for the first 12 months. She negotiated flexibility in the lease of the office. She also discussed this scenario with the bank and has some flexibility in the lending arrangement. She is far more relaxed that she could manage her way through this (while quietly confident she won't have to, based on her research).

In the "Champagne on Ice" scenario, Michelle is comfortable the bank will extend the loan arrangements and the office has plenty of capacity. She is also aware of a few other decent people she could employ in the next 12 months if things really take off. She is highly energised and believes she has the inner resilience to take on the challenges.

Therefore, by carrying out a simple scenario planning process, Michelle is committing to growth but has not been naïve enough to think that all will go to plan. As such, she is in a position to shift the plan if the future starts to match one of the scenarios she considered. She can also develop new scenarios from then on.

GOAL 6   I want to be less involved in the business —
by choice or through circumstance

At the early stages of your small business, you are likely to want to stay heavily involved in the business. In fact, you probably have little choice. As time passes, you may decide that you are less inclined to deal with the day-to-day activities or at least not feel you have given away your life to build your business.

Some long-standing businesses, especially family-owned ones, might want to hand the business to another family member (an adult child, for example). Likewise, the owner may wish to back out of the day-to-day running of the business and take up a less hands-on role.

The other less fortunate reason that may force you to back out of the business is your health or other personal reasons, which may give you little choice.

Whatever the reason, it could take a significant amount of time to prepare for this situation. I will cover some points you will need to consider if either situation eventuates.

I want to be less involved

If you have been in your small business for a long period of time, you may want to start looking at new challenges and withdraw from some aspects of the business.

A harder consideration for you might be to back away because it's in the best interests of the business. Perhaps your skills are suited to the start-up and funding stages of the business rather than for the operation of the business. Perhaps you have saturated your skills and motivation, and you need some newer, fresher ideas. Perhaps you stand to lose your successor as they see you will never vacate your role in the business (a particular issue in family businesses). This is where being self-aware is really important, as you may not wish to let go.

If you wish to withdraw from your small business, it cannot be done overnight. It's likely the business revolves around you. Preparing to withdraw from the business will be similar to the preparation you will need to do if you wanted to sell the business — it must operate without you. You will need to build this into your business planning; otherwise, the years will pass and nothing will change.

There are really only two ways this can occur and both could take some time to implement:

1. Delegate what you do to another person in the business (employee, manager, family member or partner), and
2. Develop your systems and processes to an extent that third parties can pick up the operation of business even when you are not around.

It is likely you will need a combination of both.

Delegating to a successor

Here are a few of the key questions you need to ask and answer as you consider who will start to take over the reins of your business. If the answer to any of them is no, then you have more work ahead of you. (No time like the present to start planning.)

Does anyone within your small business have the skills and desire to take over from you?

- If the answer is yes, here are a few questions you need to ask next:
  a) Does your successor share your passion for the business?
  b) Does your successor have similar values to yours?
  c) Do you and your successor have similar views on where you want the business to head?
  d) Can you define what skills your successor will need to attain to take over from you?
  e) Are you prepared to guide and mentor this person so that they can build up these skills?
  f) Do you know how long this process might take?
  g) Are you clear on what role you and your successor will take when you withdraw?
  h) Are you prepared to let your successor act independently of you? Will they have freedom to make decisions?
  i) Are you clear on what your financial position will be in your new role? Can the business afford to pay you and your successor?

- If the answer is no, your challenge is somewhat greater:
  a) Are you prepared to recruit a new person into the business who you can groom as your successor?
  b) If yes, have you anyone in mind?
  c) If you do not know of any obvious external candidates, are you clear on what you want in a new employee?

If you manage to find the right external person to take over from you, you will need to go through the same questions I asked for an internal person to prepare them. As you can imagine, this will take some time, especially if the person does not prove up to it and you have to start looking again.

If you have no obvious successor and no desire to go to the external market to find one, then you may have to simply put up with your current role in the business or sell up to escape the business.

Developing the right systems and processes

Irrespective of your desire to be less involved, every business should have appropriate processes and systems to run their business. Far too many small businesses attempt to run their business relying on the owner's memory, using paper-based processes or overly basic computer processes. There is really no reason for a business of any size to be without systems and processes appropriate for their business and their budget. There is a huge choice on the market.

If you or the members of your business have little or no computer literacy, you may decide to stay with paper-based systems. While this has limitations, it can still be done effectively. However, it requires the same disciplines, attention to detail and requirement for you to share all your information as would be the case for a computer-based system.

Even if you have a very capable successor in mind, they will be in no position to take over if everything is in your head or strewn across a disorganised set of illegible pieces of paper or documents hidden away on your computer.

You must withdraw from the business for health or personal reasons

Another potential reality is that you may be forced to take a lesser role in the business due to ill health or other unfortunate personal reasons.

If you have not prepared for this situation, you could face serious financial pressures and it could mean the end of your business. This will only add to the significant trauma that you're probably already facing.

Even if you have followed a process that allows your reduced involvement in the business, it may not remove the issue that you can no longer earn the same income as you once could.

The critical question you should ask is:

What happens if I get seriously ill and cannot work in the business?

If the closure of your business is a likely answer to this question, you need to look at your options.

☞ *Denial or 'it'll never happen to me' is not an option*

If you are in a partnership of some form, you may need to build clauses into the documents covering the business relationship. These should consider the implications of one party falling seriously ill or dying.

The other option is to look at appropriate insurance based on the risks you have considered. Insurance policies and processes vary. There will be a form of insurance to cover the business risks you may face. The issue is how much you will have to pay to insure against any given risk.

The following are some typical examples that exist to cover ill health in your business.

- **Income Protection:** This provides the holder with a source of income should they fall seriously ill and become unable to work in their normal role. These may have a finite period to give you time to return to work.

- **Key Personnel Insurance:** This insures the business should key members (such as the owner or a key manager) fall seriously ill or die.
- **Trauma Insurance:** This covers an individual should they become permanently disabled and unable to work.
- **Life Insurance:** In the case of the owner's death, life insurance may allow the surviving partner to continue operating the business.
- **Loan Protection Insurance:** This is designed to help provide you with financial support to cover loan repayments in times of need.
- **Revenue Protection Insurance:** This provides you with cover should you suffer any injury or illness and are unable to work. This benefit can be used to pay for any business expenses like staff wages, buildings or utilities.

The best advice is to find a good insurance broker. Look for someone who is not linked to a specific insurance company so they can offer you the best independent proposal.

Remember, insurance is simply a means to manage your risk. The hope is you never need to call on it. However, if the risk eventuates and you have done nothing to protect yourself, you could be in very serious trouble.

GOAL 7   I must close the business

The process ('goal' is perhaps a misplaced term in this case.) of closing your small business may be a serious option that you can't ignore. It is likely to be your last resort.

Failure in numbers

The failure of small businesses is an all-too-common occurrence. Not surprisingly, the vast majority of businesses that start up in any year are small businesses. Unfortunately, they are also the most likely to fail, if not in the first year, certainly within five years.

This is borne out in the statistics, which show similar trends the world over:

- Statistics New Zealand stated that, in 2012, 84% of small businesses survive the first year but only 27% survive until the tenth year. The smaller you are, the bigger risk you have, statistically, of failing. From 2009 to 2012, only 53% of 'non-employing' businesses in New Zealand survived and only 31% of businesses with one to five employees survived. However, 94% of companies with more than 50 employees survived the same period.
- The Australian Bureau of Statistics indicates that, in 2010–11, 76,000 business with fewer than four employees entered the marketplace but 48,000 exited.
- The USA's Small Business Association statistics state that 533,000 businesses came into being in 2012, 515,000 having fewer than 20 employees. In the same year, more businesses ceased to exist than started, 593,000. Of those 593,000 businesses that died, 572,000 had fewer than 20 employees.
- The UK Office of National Statistics indicates that the five-year survival rate of

businesses born in 2007 was only 45%, whereas 95% survived the first year and 81% the second year.

You may be tempted to debate the intricacies of this small statistical sample. Benjamin Disraeli, the United Kingdom's Prime Minister in the late 1800s, made his views on statistics well known:

There are three types of lies: lies, damned lies, and statistics.

No matter which statistic is pursued, the message that keeps coming up in almost every country is that there are many small businesses that start in any given year. Several may last a year or two, but more than half of them fail by the fifth year. The smaller your business, the more likely it is to fail. While I hope you never need to consider this option, many of the most successful businesspeople have had to take this action, as these sobering statistics would indicate. And so, we need to cover it here.

Reasons for closing

If you are forced to leave the business due to factors outside your control and can still sell the business as a going concern, then you should still attempt to get the best price you can.

Typical reasons you could be forced out include:

- You or your family strike health issues.
- You have had enough and want your old life back.
- You decide to return to paid employment.
- You have to leave your current location for other reasons.
- It no longer meets your expectations.

The less appealing reasons for closure, which are sadly far too common, are:

- You fear if you don't act, your creditors, those who you owe money, including the tax department, suppliers or bank, will step in. This means you want to declare voluntary liquidation and manage the closure.
- Your creditors may step in via the courts. In the first instance, if they see their money is at risk, they may call in a receiver. This is done if the creditor has security over some assets. The most common example is a bank. They will get the receiver to see what money can be recovered before the business is liquidated.
- The more common situation with small businesses is that they are forced directly into liquidation.

Liquidation can be triggered if you are insolvent and feel you have saturated all other options to return to solvency. The typical definition of insolvency is that you are unable to pay your debts when they fall due.

The liquidation process and the roles of different parties, including your role and the court's, will differ from country to country. However, the process comes back to some simple yet very unpleasant realities.

If you realise you can't pay your creditors, you can either choose to act or wait until they act. Your creditors will want to be paid the money they are legally entitled to and may do all they can to get that money. Who leads this process and what assets creditors can access to get this money may differ.

No matter where in the world liquidations occur, it is an extremely painful, long and unpleasant process.

Who gets what

The order of priority for the creditors that get your funds following liquidation will vary from country to country. Typically, the parties to get paid after your business's assets have been liquidated will be those who were given security over those assets. The people put in place to carry out the liquidation and to distribute funds will have a high priority (the liquidators). Some countries have wages and any pension funds as the next priority after secured creditors (e.g. Australia and the USA). Last are the unsecured creditors like your suppliers and shareholders (including you). It is unlikely employees and unsecured creditors will get anything.

The reality is, if you are liquidated, there may not be enough to pay secured creditors, let alone unsecured creditors.

If it feels as if this process is a little like the vultures picking at the carcass of what was your business, you have good reason; none of those to whom you owe money will feel the slightest concern for you. In fact, don't be surprised if you are confronted with hostility, especially from those who have a lower priority over your money, including your suppliers and staff. They have their own lives and businesses to run and you owe them money.

What risks do you face if your business is liquidated?

If you are facing the liquidation of your business, the emotional and financial impacts that this brings may only be the start of your problems.

While the laws may vary in different countries, you could face serious legal implications if you knowingly continue to operate your business when it was clear you could not pay your creditors. In a number of jurisdictions, this is called 'trading while insolvent' or 'wrongful trading'. Therefore, the risk of legal action against you may exist.

The other risk is what you personally stand to lose following the liquidation of your business. This is why you need to fully understand the extent of your liabilities. The company structure you have chosen is also critical. If you own a limited liability company and you have given no personal guarantee over any of your personal assets, your liabilities are likely to be limited to your business.

If, however, your bank or other supplier secured what they have borrowed based on a personal guarantee from you, then they may be able to attack your assets to recover their money.

If you are a sole proprietor, you are legally liable for everything and could have your assets seized to pay off debts.

How can you avoid liquidation?

Cash is always king. If you start seeing an ongoing slide in the cash in your bank account, if you are struggling more often to pay your suppliers on time, or if your bank is indicating concerns, you must act.

You need to act early. With a fresh set of eyes there may be a number of actions that can be taken to help you survive. These could be really unpleasant (e.g. laying off longstanding employees to whom you are very close). This is why a trusted advisor could be critical to have beside you.

Communicate with your suppliers, the tax department or your bank if you are struggling to meet your obligations to them. Even if you are in trouble and can't pay suppliers in the short term, they may prefer to establish new payment terms to assist in your recovery. It is in their interest to see you survive. If you have very poor relationships with these people, they may show little sympathy. If you have been a good payer over a long period, this may give you a better chance of getting support when you can't pay on time.

If you do fail to act early, your bank or other funder may not want to lend you any more money. Your suppliers will put you under significant pressure to pay or stop supplying you. If your cash reserves have dried up, with little immediate signs of increased sales, then all these combined factors could mean you are likely to be out of options. People may also be less inclined to help because they know they are unlikely to get paid to help you. It is a bit like calling the fire brigade when the house is almost burnt to the ground.

While you may not want to consider liquidation until it's your last option, you should still seek some advice on what is involved if it is becoming a possibility. The laws in some countries offer options that may give you some hope. For example, in the United Kingdom, there are options that allow you to remain involved in the business and attempt to trade your way out of the situation.

How does the 'failure' of your business make you feel?

"Remember that failure is an event, not a person."
— Zig Ziglar, American author, salesman, and motivational speaker

If, through all the best efforts of you and external people, you're unable to keep the business going, how will you feel?

This is the situation where you will be least able to see any success. It can be devastating. While you are unlikely to see it when it occurs, with time, I hope you will see that you can come back and try again.

You need to remember that just because the business may have 'failed', it does not mean you are a failure.

It is at times like this in business where the resilience you have built up and the relationships you have carved out will be most critical. No matter how strong you think you are, these can be extremely tough times. Hang in there. Seek the support of those close to you. Talk about it. There is always light at the end of the tunnel.

Summary

Some closing comments on your long-term goals:

- From the day you start your small business, you will need to have some idea of the long-term goal or you will simply drift along.
- As you, your business and the world changes, so too might your goals. Make these changes mindfully and not at the behest of other forces around you.
- Write down your goals. They are more likely to happen.
- Consider some of the most common small business goals. Do any of these align with your goal?
  - a) Start a new business
  - b) Be more profitable
  - c) Buy a business
  - d) Grow your business
  - e) Remove yourself from the business
  - f) Sell the business
  - g) Close the business
- Once you have established your goal, you are able to start planning how you will deliver on this goal.

Questions

- What generic goal best represents where you want your business to be in the next three to five years?
- What other goals do you have for your business?

Chapter 8
Reaching Your Customers — Your Marketing

What does marketing mean to you?

When I ask small business owners what marketing is to them, I get very different responses. Typical answers include that it is 'advertising', it's 'a web page', it's 'promoting my products', it's 'cold-calling', it's 'selling', and so on.

The American Marketing Association defines 'marketing' as:

> *"the activity, set of institutions, and processes for creating, communicating, delivering, and exchanging offerings that have value for customers, clients, partners, and society at large".*

Your business is being marketed whether you do so consciously or not. Every time you discuss your business, sell a product or service or come into touch with the world around you, marketing is happening for your business. How well you are being marketed and how people receive your marketing is quite a different thing.

Marketing is a process that anyone can develop, and then deliver for their business, no matter how small they are. It's not some nebulous concept that requires a unique creative gift. As the definition states, it involves communication. When I say communication, it is the process of breaking through the noise and reaching those you wish to communicate with, namely your customers, either existing or new. It is about selling your product or service and ultimately doing the entire process in a way that makes you some money.

For many small businesses, with little or no experience in marketing, the process of pushing their products, services and entire business can be very daunting. You may feel quite excited about the prospect of putting yourself out there, promoting what you do, what you sell and chasing potential customers. However, you may also feel petrified about the whole idea of doing this and find selling yourself and your product or services a really uncomfortable process. Many hate networking and cold-calling, but the days of putting an advert in the *Yellow Pages* and waiting for the calls to roll in are long gone. Getting customers is hard work. This is why, as a small business, when you do get a customer, it is so rewarding. And so important to look after them.

Who are your ideal customers?

Your entire marketing plan and processes should be centred on the most fundamental thing: your customers. This may seem inherent and obvious, but we can get tied up in our day-to-day business life and lose sight of our customers.

Before getting into any marketing process, answer this question:

Who are your ideal customers?

If you are going to devote your limited marketing resources to anyone, it should be on those you believe to be your ideal customers. This is not a one-off process. Your customers' habits and needs will change; the products and services you offer may change. If you are an established business, you must continually assess what your customers are saying.

Start by establishing as much information as you can about your ideal customers so you can choose the best and lowest cost methods to reach and engage with them. Here is a range of things you might consider:

- How old are they?
- Where do they live?
- What income might they have to spend?
- What do they read, watch and listen to?
- Where do they spend their free time?
- Where do they like to buy products? Online, in supermarkets, high-end shopping centres or malls?
- How might your product or service improve their day-to-day lives?
- Where do they congregate?

And so on.

What makes your business different?

To an uninitiated customer, your business may look exactly the same as your competitors. What you sell or what you do might appear identical. You may be one of a dozen plumbers in a town. You may be a small accountant in a place with many other accountants.

What makes you different from these businesses? Why would a customer choose you rather than one of the many other businesses that do what you do? Can you answer the following question if asked by a potential customer?

Why should I use you rather than your competitor?

This is a critical question that you need to be able to answer without hesitation. If you can't answer it, how can you expect a customer to see it and choose you?

This is called your **Point of Difference**. Can you clearly distinguish what sets you apart from other businesses like you? Have you got a unique selling point? When people hear your business's name, what will spring into their minds?

If your only point of difference is price, you need to be cautious. As a small business, the depth of your finances is unlikely to sustain an attack from a larger business keen to steal your customers. Your point of difference needs to offer something that builds loyalty. Price is only one factor in the decision to buy from you. A focused and differentiated message has a better chance of breaking through the clutter and being remembered. Revisit your purpose, because this is part of what makes you different from others.

This differentiation is more likely to see you attract and keep more loyal customers, as you offer them something special that your competitors don't.

What is your 'brand'?

Typically, when someone mentions the word 'brand' many people consider a business's logo. However, brand is far more than this. Seth Godin defines it as:

The set of expectations, memories, stories and relationships that, taken together, account for a consumer's decision to choose one product or service over another.

As with marketing, you are creating a 'brand' around you and your business whether you are doing it consciously or not. People will be forming a view of you and your business based on how you hold yourself, how you interact with them, what you say and what you do. We discussed your point of difference as part of your strategy. This is very much tied to your brand. When someone thinks of you or your business, or sees your logo, what thoughts come to his or her mind?

Your brand is intangible. You cannot touch or hold it. It exists only in the minds of your customers. Your brand is far more than a logo. It is absolutely intertwined with your core purpose and values. The way you and your team behave around customers, suppliers and other external parties will contribute to the brand they perceive. The logo simply identifies you. What people feel about you and how they want to engage with you will depend on your brand, not the logo. It is simple things that form in people's minds like "Don't call those guys; they never call you back" or "That lady tells a great story about her business, but that's not how she delivers her service".

You will have a reputation. You have no choice about that. Where you do have a choice is what kind of reputation you want and what efforts you put in to develop that reputation.

As the owner of a small business, your personal brand and your business's brand are so related that they could well be the same thing.

In their book *The Human Brand*, Chris Malone and Susan Fiske discuss two factors that contribute to your small business's brand. They are your **warmth** and your **competence**.

- **Warmth** will be judged by assessing whether you are kind, friendly and good-natured; whether you appear sincere, honest, moral and trustworthy; whether you possess an accommodating orientation; whether you are perceived as being helpful, tolerant, fair, generous and understanding.
- **Competence** is judged by assessing whether you are efficient, capable, skilful and clever enough to successfully carry out your intentions towards your customer in either the services you offer or the products you provide. Contributing to competence are your strength, status, resourcefulness, skills, creativity and intelligence.

All the marketing in the world won't replace the substance of you and your business. This includes the clarity of your purpose and point of difference. It includes knowing what you stand for and the behaviour you demonstrate. Finally, your business's brand is reflected in the warmth you show your customers and your competence to deliver.

The Four Ps of marketing

Before we get into the specifics of what you can do to reach your customers, let's look at some of the basics of marketing.

Edmund Jerome McCarthy put forward in his 1960 book *Basic Marketing — A Managerial Approach* his view that there are four fundamental variables that marketing needs to consider. These are the Four Ps of marketing. McCarthy's concept, while over 50 years old, is as relevant today as it was then.

The Four Ps are:

1. **PRODUCT**
2. **PRICE**
3. **PLACE**
4. **PROMOTION**

Over the last few decades, people have refined and added to these Four Ps including

Positioning, People and Packaging. However, the original Four Ps are still an excellent place to start when considering your sales and marketing strategies.

1. Your Product

People don't buy your product or service; they buy the benefits it brings to their lives. These benefits can come in many forms.

If your product or service does not help or solve your customer's issues or problems, then you will really struggle as a business, no matter how good the rest of your business is run.

In his book *Buyology*, Martin Lindstrom discussed the challenges faced by businesses trying to establish why people make certain purchasing decisions. Most of us struggle to really pin down the basis of some of our purchasing decisions. We don't really know why we choose to buy one item or brand over another. We are often very poor at understanding our own actions and then explaining them. This will make it difficult for you as the seller of a product or service to predict what your customers are likely to do when they probably don't know anyway.

Lindstrom goes on to say that tests using fMRI (functional Magnetic Resonance Imaging), which monitors brain activity, demonstrated that our purchasing decisions (in fact, most of our decisions) are not driven by rational thought processes, but by our emotions. Our decisions are also filtered through our personal biases, cultural traditions, upbringing, and many other subconscious factors that we don't even recognise are influencing why we buy what we do.

This does challenge the idea that asking potential customers what their actions might be, in market research, will answer your questions. As a small business owner you are also unlikely to have the resources to carry out any sizeable research anyway. The best and lowest cost option may simply be to get the product out into the market as inexpensively as you can and see what the response is. You can continue to revise and adjust your offering based on the response.

2. Your Pricing

Determining the price for your product or service can be a challenge, especially for a start-up or when you are selling a unique product or service. There are a few important things to consider in pricing:

a) Is your product or service unique?
b) How important is pricing in differentiating you from others?
c) What are your closest competitors' prices?
d) What does it cost to produce your product or service?
e) What value does the customer believe they are receiving from your product or service?

a) Unique product or service

If you are confident your product is unique or offers something for your customers that no-one else can offer, you're in a strong position to push your prices up. You still need to be cautious that you are not becoming excessive in your pricing, because if you exceed the value the customer believes they are getting from your product, they may simply choose to go without.

It is also very unlikely that any product or service you produce will remain unique for long. Even if you have protected the intellectual property of your product or service, if it's in demand, someone will find a way to replicate it and eat into your market.

b) Price versus loyalty

As a small business, it is very unlikely you will ever be able to compete with bigger businesses solely on the basis of price. They are likely to have much deeper pockets and the capacity to undercut you and even run at a loss to strangle you. Instead, you have to offer more than price so you can build up strong loyalty with customers.

If you do this, it is far less likely that customers will move if a lower cost option comes their way. Businesses that compete solely on price are really only selling a commodity: a product or service that has no distinguishing difference except price; where people will simply go to the seller who offers the best price.

c) Competitors' prices

Every customer will have a point where their loyalty is tested if the price difference with your nearest competitors is too great. If your product or service is not unique, you ought to monitor the pricing activity of your nearest competitors. While you may not follow the changes they make in their pricing, you at least need to know exactly where you are relative to them.

It's also worth remembering that you may believe your competitor is the store down the street. It may actually be the business on the other side of the world selling into your region via the internet. Spend some time online determining who all your competitors are.

d) Cost of making your product or service

There is little point reducing the price of your product to such an extent that you are not making money selling it. While this would appear to be a self-evident point, far too many small businesses don't fully understand the cost involved in producing each of their products or services.

We will discuss the concepts of fixed and variable costs as well as gross profit in much greater detail in later chapters. For now, you need to carefully consider what it costs to produce each individual product and also the additional fixed costs (or overheads) that you have (for example, your rent, paying off your mortgage).

If you make short-term decisions to lower your prices on the basis of competitor behaviour, you could find yourself in a lot of trouble. You may well sell more and appear to be making more money, but by the time you take out all your costs, you might not be in great shape.

e) Price versus value

There is a view that the price you charge customers should not reflect the cost to produce the product or service but the value it adds to the customer. The key point to remember is the value added to the customer may be quite subjective. The only relevant consideration is what the customer perceives to be the value. This can be difficult to gauge especially since decisions by customers are not always rational.

If your business is service-based and you are selling your time, this can be particularly difficult. Selling your time solely on an hourly rate basis can create issues, because hourly rates measure only your input, the hours *you* put in. They don't measure the value the customer will get out of this time. It also allows the customer to compare you with other people in unrelated businesses based solely on a dollars-per-hour rate.

For example, a customer could ask the following question about three services they receive:

> *Why does my accountant charge $150/hour, my tradesmen $65/hour, but my lawyer $300/hour?*

If this customer had a burst water pipe, $65/hour is amazing value for them. If someone was suing this same individual, all of a sudden $300/hour seems really good value.

If you offer a service, there is a risk that time may be what your customers think you are selling. However, it is your skill, expertise and experience and the value that you bring that your customer is paying for.

Your time will always be limited. You can only work so many hours in a week and rarely can you charge for all those hours. As a result, you can probably work out the maximum income you will ever make using a model based solely on hourly rates.

Make every effort to price the value you add, not the hours you put in. It may take time for you to understand your market and test its boundaries. You will also find different customers will have very different views of the value you add, even if they receive the same service from you. There is a point where you simply need to hold your ground and say no to those who undervalue what you offer.

Some examples of pricing mark-ups

It is interesting to look at some of the mark-ups you may be paying on some well-known products. The fact that we keep buying these products must mean we see value in them well beyond the cost to produce them. These are examples where we are clearly prepared to pay much more based on the perceived value rather than the actual cost.

- Movie theatre popcorn has an average mark-up of more than 1,000%.
- Diamonds have a mark-up of up to 400%.
- The average mark-up on cosmetics is around 78%.
- Printer ink and toner for your computer's printer is among the costliest substances you can buy. The printers typically sell at a loss. The ink sells for around $US 4,000/litre.

- Bottled water costs about $US 0.001/litre to produce, but sells for around $ 2–4 a bottle.
- Electronics products, while in a very competitive market, still produce good margins for the leading suppliers Apple and Samsung. For example, the Samsung Galaxy 10.1 notepad costs about $ 300 to make but, depending on where you are, costs around $ 620 to buy.

3. Your Place

When Edmund Jerome McCarthy first put forward the concept of the Four Ps in 1960, the internet was still more than 30 years away. Global internet sales grew to $US 1,250 billion by 2013 and are predicted to continue growing every year. Even so, they are still a fraction of the sales that occur through traditional bricks-and-mortar shops. In addition, many businesses online also have a bricks-and-mortar presence.

There is no question that the internet offers your small business access to markets that 20 years ago would have been beyond your reach. Therefore, we will devote more detailed attention to marketing and selling through the internet shortly. However, the internet does not remove the huge number of solo and small businesses whose sales are still based solely on being in a physical location.

Your choice of location may have been determined by factors other than what best suits your business. Your business location may be dictated by the town where you live, where your kids go to school, where your family is located, where your husband, wife or partner works, or any number of other reasons.

Even within these restrictions, there are still many factors you should consider before deciding on a final location to set up your store or office. Here are a few considerations:

- **Customers.** The most critical consideration on the location you choose is reaching your customers. There's not much point being in a location that's convenient for you if it's inconvenient for your customers.
- **Costs.** Remember you are small, so you have much greater flexibility to choose low-cost places to reside. For example, if you can base yourself at home, it will substantially reduce your fixed costs.
- **Space and capacity.** If you choose inadequate space to save costs, it could prove to be a false economy, especially if your goal is growth.
- **Competition.** Depending on your particular business, you may wish to locate adjacent to competitors, to feed off their customers, or as far away as possible.
- **Suppliers.** If you are heavily reliant on certain suppliers and their speed and availability of response, you may need to be nearby.
- **Staff.** If you do have a few employees, you will need to consider their needs.
- **Brand image.** If you have an image you want to portray, your location may enhance or undermine this.

Where you have the option to choose your location, do your homework. Getting it wrong could be very costly. Firstly and most importantly, ask yourself what location will best serve your customers and make it easy for them to find you.

If you are already in a location, but not satisfied with it, the decision to move may be a critical one. It is most likely to be a trade-off between the increase in sales you hope to achieve and the costs to relocate. If your current location is restricting your business from achieving the purpose you have set and the goals you want to achieve, you should seriously consider a move, or be left with regrets of what might have been.

4. Your Promotion

This is the P that most people associate with marketing — promoting your product or service through some form of advertising.

The amount of money spent on advertising that is directed at you is borne out in the highest per-capita advertising spenders in the world:

- Australia — $ 582 (per person)
- UK — $ 540
- Norway — $ 535
- USA — $ 404
- Denmark — $ 397

A quick check of the population in each country will give you some sense of the money spent trying to get you to buy a company's goods and services. In Australia, that's about $US 13 billion and in the USA it's about $US 150 billion.

> *"Advertising expenditures have been rising continually, totalling, in 1958, approximately $ 10 billion."*
> — **Edmund Jerome McCarthy**, *Basic Marketing — A Managerial Approach* (1960)

It seems the rising cost of advertising has not slowed since McCarthy's 1958 statistics.

These are pretty scary numbers when we flash back to the type of average earnings small businesses make in total, let alone how much we can set aside for marketing. It may also give you some sense of the extent to which companies are prepared to go to attract attention, given our attention is limited and we can only take in so much. Considering the bombardment that is coming from the well-resourced companies, how can you possibly break through the noise and engage with your customers?

In short, you will need to be far more analytical about who your ideal customers are and how you can reach them at the lowest cost. Also be prepared to experiment. Adapt your promotional methods or risk wasting your limited resources.

☞ *The most expensive advertising may not be the most effective for a small business. The best advertising might cost you nothing but will cost you time. The best advertising might be just you getting out and meeting people, talking about your business.*

Have you got a marketing problem or a brand problem?

When you are pondering your next marketing steps, it's worth asking yourself the following question if you're not selling at the levels you believe you should be.

Have I got a marketing problem or a brand problem?

If too few people know about you, you have a marketing problem. If you believe there are many potential customers who do know about you but choose your competitors, then it's likely you have an issue with your brand. In short, that means you're not getting it quite right and that's turning off potential customers.

The more likely problem of the two for a small business is the former: a marketing problem, where you simply don't have the resources to reach all your potential customers.

The Marketing Funnel

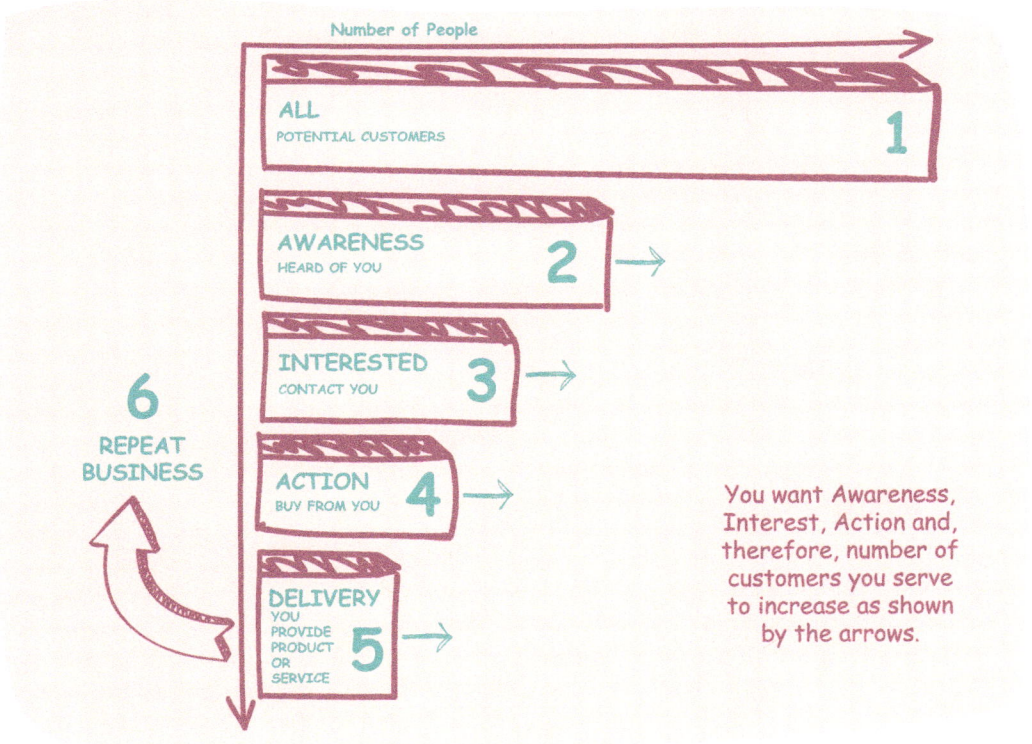

Number of People

ALL POTENTIAL CUSTOMERS — 1

AWARENESS HEARD OF YOU — 2

INTERESTED CONTACT YOU — 3

6 **REPEAT BUSINESS**

ACTION BUY FROM YOU — 4

DELIVERY YOU PROVIDE PRODUCT OR SERVICE — 5

You want Awareness, Interest, Action and, therefore, number of customers you serve to increase as shown by the arrows.

Fig. 5: The Marketing Funnel

As far back as 1898, Elias St Elmo Lewis raised the concept of a customer's journey from becoming aware of a brand and developing an interest in it, before having the desire to act and purchase. This is often called the Purchasing or Marketing Funnel.

Let's take this concept and expand it a little, as it relates to your small business. Consider the funnel for your business as a graph like that shown in Figure 5 on the previous page.

The impetus of your marketing efforts is described in each bar of The Marketing Funnel. These are:

1. Identify all your potential customers (group 1 in Figure 3).
2. Find the best way to engage with these potential customers at a budget you can afford so they have at least heard of you. This is likely to be a much smaller number of people than in 1.
3. Once they have heard of you, attempt to spark enough interest so you will get them to take further steps or at least engage with you at a later date. This will be a smaller number of people than in 2.
4. Continue this process until there is a sufficient call to action to get them to act. This will be a smaller number of people than in 3.
5. After all this effort, if you gain a customer, do everything you can to deliver the product or service as best you can. You want to maximise the number of leads from group 4 that convert into customers. This will only occur if you increase the number who have heard of you and then acted to find out about you.
6. If this occurs, it is very likely you will see that customer again or they will give you a referral.

☞ *A Nielsen report in 2013 called the 'Global Trust in Advertising and Brand Messages' highlighted that referrals are the most trusted form of advertising there is. It is also the form of advertising that will most likely turn into a purchase.*

You should always attempt, through your marketing, to lift the number of people in groups 2, 3 and 4 so that you will see more conversions to customers.

Traditional methods of promoting your business

If you are reasonably clear who your ideal customers are, you can start to consider how best to reach them at a price you can afford. While I will devote more attention to online marketing, traditional means of promoting your business are still very relevant.

The Nielsen report 'Global Trust in Advertising and Brand Messages' found through their surveys that traditional forms of advertising are still some of the most trusted forms of advertising and most likely to convert into sales.

Here are some of the traditional means you may wish to consider and some of the advantages and disadvantages of each. Just remember, the key is still that you know your customers, and which form of marketing will most effectively reach them.

Trying to target an 18-year-old girl through a newspaper is unlikely to work too well. Teenagers are using the internet to watch video material far more than television, so television may not be the means to reach them any more either.

No matter what medium you choose, you need to consider the fundamentals. Who are my customers? How do I best reach them? How can I test that this promotion has delivered the return on investment that I was seeking?

Advertising Medium	Advantages	Disadvantages
Television	▪ One of the most trusted forms of advertising. ▪ Highly engaging. ▪ Huge reach. ▪ Uses audio and video. ▪ Uses specific times and stations to target audience. ▪ Strong conversion into sales.	▪ Expensive and outside the reach of most small businesses. ▪ Complex to develop. ▪ Very short and difficult to portray all information. ▪ Needs to be repeated many times. ▪ It is very difficult to assess who has seen it, who can recall it and who has taken action as a result without additional market research.
Radio	▪ Lower cost than television. ▪ Can be produced quickly. ▪ Allows targeting through different stations and time slots. ▪ Strong local presence.	▪ While lower cost than TV still out of the reach of many small businesses. ▪ Cannot refer back to adverts. ▪ Radio is often background noise. ▪ Tends to interrupt entertainment. ▪ Need to be repeated many times. ▪ It is very difficult to assess who has seen it, who can recall it and who has acted as a result without additional market research.

Billboards	<ul><li>They will be seen as they are placed in strategic locations.</li><li>You can place your advertisement in a location that best aligns with your business.</li><li>Most locations will have good information on the number of vehicles that pass the point.</li><li>Has the potential to be seen numerous times by a potential customer.</li></ul>	<ul><li>Messages must be brief.</li><li>You cannot filter out to the demographics you are targeting — only volumes of cars.</li><li>You may be required to post your advertisement for a minimum time period even if it is not working.</li><li>Risk of vandalism.</li><li>Stationary images with no sound or movement.</li><li>Difficult to assess who has seen it, who can recall it and who has taken action as a result without additional market research.</li></ul>
Mailbox Flyer Drops	<ul><li>Low cost to produce and deliver.</li><li>Can be very specific on the geographical area you wish to target.</li><li>Easy and quick to read and establish the message.</li><li>Easy to produce and reproduce.</li><li>Effective, as only a small number of successful responses are needed to cover the costs (e.g. real estates drop thousands of flyers; they only need one house sale to cover all costs).</li></ul>	<ul><li>Difficult to assess who has seen it, who can recall it and who has acted as a result without additional market research.</li><li>Easily dismissed by customers (often thrown out).</li><li>Limited long-term impact.</li><li>Difficult to establish the demographics within a household.</li><li>Very low conversion to sales so each sale must be worthwhile.</li></ul>

Cinema Advertising	■ Captive audience. ■ Allows sound and movement. ■ Big screen can enhance a lower-budget advertisement. ■ The advertisements can narrow in on target audiences, based on the movie and its rating. ■ Usually cheaper than TV advertising.	■ Difficult to assess who has seen it, who can recall it and who has acted as a result without additional market research. ■ People know that advertisements before movies can be long and can stay outside the theatre and fail to see the advertisement.
Newspapers (paper based)	■ One advertisement can access a very large readership. ■ Can align your message with the appropriate readership and sections within the newspaper. ■ Relatively simple to produce. ■ More newspapers are going online.	■ Difficult to assess who has seen it, who can recall it and who has acted as a result without additional market research. ■ A medium that has seen significant competition and declines in readership. ■ Static image. ■ Short life span. ■ Low younger readership. ■ Can be expensive.
Magazines (paper based)	■ The variety of magazines allows very targeted campaigns, across a wide demographic. ■ Readership numbers are usually well known. ■ More magazines are going online. ■ Able to access a very wide geographical readership. ■ Much longer shelf-life than a newspaper.	■ Difficult to assess who has seen it, who can recall it and who has acted as a result without additional market research. ■ Market flooded with a huge variety of magazine titles. ■ Typically monthly prints so there could be a long time between deciding to advertise and reaching print. ■ Can be expensive. ■ A medium that has seen significant competition and declining readership.

Online marketing

Online sales exceeded $US 1,250 billion worldwide in 2013; Amazon alone contributed $US 68 billion of this. In the USA, 191 million people shop online.

Considering the first online sale only occurred in the mid-1980s, internet-based shopping comprises a significant change in purchasing behaviour.

For small businesses like yours, it offers unprecedented options to reach customers and markets that would have been totally out of your reach in the last decade.

Online marketing also offers very detailed analytics about who has interacted with your business. As all actions by online users can be tracked and recorded, you can receive very fast and accurate feedback on what marketing has worked and what hasn't. You can see what pages people have visited on your website, how long they stayed, where they came from, what order they visited and so on. This is one of the most significant advantages of online marketing over traditional forms of marketing for small business. In the past, you would not have had the resources to research the effectiveness of your marketing campaigns that online marketing allows today.

The growth of online marketing and sales has brought about a huge industry of business support companies to maximise the benefits of their online presence. It is not my intention to cover the required details that allow you to implement your online presence. I won't tell you how to design your webpage, or your LinkedIn or Facebook profile, nor how to achieve the best Search Engine Optimisation (SEO).

My aim here is to simply guide you towards the best mix of marketing options to align with your goals for the business. If an online presence meets these needs based on what we discuss below, which I am confident it will, then I strongly recommend you seek out the best advice you can afford that supports your skill set.

If you are a heavy online and social media user with strong IT skills, there is an endless supply of material to help you develop your own online presence with minimal external help. If this is not your forte, there are many options available to get the help you need, hopefully at a price you can afford. I am certainly the latter of these groups and have called on the support of website developers and social media experts to guide me. With time, I am becoming more and more comfortable with how powerful online marketing is, but the pace of change is still likely to outstrip my knowledge and I will continue seeking external expertise.

Don't underestimate the amount of work maintaining a high-quality online presence might take. Once you have built a website, entered the social media world or blogged, you are unlikely to start seeing much of an increase in sales from day one. It's not that simple. You need to continually make efforts to connect with your potential customers. It may take many connections with a potential customer before they act to connect with you and then buy from you.

The importance of your online content

The key purpose of the content you put online is to attract and retain customers by providing them with relevant and valuable information. Whether it is written information, diagrams, illustrations, video or audio, it must add value. If done well, the content can also tell a story about your business. It can also be a call to action for those watching or reading the content. Educate the viewer.

The development of quality online content is called **content marketing**.

One of the challenges of content marketing is that it requires you to volunteer a lot of free information. However, if the reader gets value from that information, it raises your perceived competence. If the quality of your online content is high, it will increase the trust readers have in you. They are more likely to visit again (and again), if done well, essentially giving you permission to engage with them.

In developing any content (both online and in other offline literature), first stop and ask yourself if that content will genuinely help your customer. They, like you, are very time-poor. If your interaction only plugs your business and is of little value to the reader, you may see that your newsletter quickly finds its way into the bin or the person is already on another website.

Your website

In 2013, there were approximately 675 million websites and more than 2.7 billion internet users. This is up from about 350 million websites in 2011. This is even more amazing considering the first website only came into existence in 1991. By 1997, there were still fewer than 2 million websites.

With this much traffic, building your website could simply be like putting a small sign in the middle of the Amazon jungle and hoping people see it.

While being online is now almost a given for any business, it requires effort to make it work for you. It needs to fit in with your business's broader strategy. You must understand why you are doing it, and how it will achieve your three- to five-year goal. It is a window from the world into your business. It may be the only connection between you and potential customers, so it needs to reflect well on who you are, what you stand for and your point of difference.

Whether you decide to build a website yourself or use the experts, spend the time and money getting it right and making sure you can be proud of it. A poorly presented and cheap-looking website will reflect negatively on your business and on you.

Get clear on what you hope to achieve from your website.

If your business is local to a small region and most of your customers come through word of mouth or from a demographic with low internet use, you may not need to invest significant effort in a website. However, if you rely heavily on it to attract new customers and sell to them online, you should expect to devote significantly more time to achieve the reach you are seeking.

Getting on page one of Google

Your website may be there to validate who you are with customers who already know about you. It might also be your primary means to be found by new customers or to connect with existing customers. In either case, you should still apply some simple methods to increase your chances of being found.

If the primary reason for your website is to attract customers and entice them to follow your marketing funnel through your website to the point where you make a sale (either online or through your physical store), you will need to think in far more detail about how to develop your website.

Search Engine Optimisation (SEO) techniques and the requirements to be found change continually and rapidly. Maintaining expertise on the best SEO techniques requires specialist knowledge. Some of the basic techniques to increase your chances of forcing your way up the rankings are:

- Choose keywords throughout your website that are most likely to be what a person will choose when looking for what you are selling.
- Use keywords in natural phrasing and use them a lot throughout the website.
- Provide high-quality content on your website. Make it information-rich.
- Update your content regularly.
- Give all your web pages descriptive names as Google often displays search results as a link to the page title.
- The more interconnected your website is with other websites, the more highly ranked it is likely to be.
- The more highly ranked the website that refers to you is, the better your ranking will be.
- When connecting with other websites, use hyperlink titles that are descriptive and consistent with keywords.
- A well-designed website with well-organised pages will tend to rank more highly.
- The more popular your website becomes, the higher ranked you will become.

☞ *Remember, search engines like Google change their processes and this world is very dynamic. You need to continually review and refine the best techniques to be found.*

The more computer-savvy you are, the more you can dig into the background of your website to optimise it. For those less capable, talk to your web developer.

I believe even if you are an expert you should still turn to external people, at least to offer you an independent set of eyes on your website design. If this is your main medium to connect with current and future customers, it must be done exceptionally well.

Mobile devices

With the rapid increase in mobile devices it is now extremely easy for a customer to find what they are looking for through a search from a smartphone or tablet. By the end of 2013, there were more mobile devices on Earth than people.

Mobile devices are now the starting point of most internet searches and also where a spontaneous purchase will most likely occur. In designing your website, therefore, consider making it mobile- as well as computer-friendly.

Again, to reinforce the point about knowing your ideal customer, if your customers are very unlikely to ever use a smartphone, mobile-friendliness may not be so critical.

Permission marketing

Seth Godin in his book *Permission Marketing* put forward his view that, in the online world, businesses need to move away from traditional marketing techniques to **permission marketing**.

A business normally forces its way into your life through a TV or radio advertisement, an internet pop-up or banner, billboard or any of the numerous approaches we are used to seeing. This is called **interruption marketing**. The hope for a business using this technique is that the interruption will catch your attention and result in you taking some action. The billions of dollars that go into advertising are usually based on this technique.

Seth Godin believes we should be doing more to get the permission of potential customers to start a relationship with them. Over time, this will hopefully lead to sales.

The idea is to get potential customers to give you their contact details so that you can build a relationship with them. Most customers will protect these details (a little like they protect their wallets) and are unlikely to hand over their details unless they feel they are receiving something in exchange. In your online activity, you are strongly advised to offer future customers something of value, in order to gain their details and consequent permission to interact.

While I believe you will need to consider traditional interruption marketing, you're likely to have much greater success if you can build a relationship with your potential customers so they want to use you, rather than pushing yourself on them. Besides, you are unlikely to have the resources to get the traction through traditional forms of interruption marketing.

Email marketing

Another very powerful form of online marketing is email marketing. This is where you engage directly with existing customers or potential customers using email communication. While you can do this on an email-by-email basis there are some excellent email marketing tools on the market that can do large numbers of emails automatically. (Two systems I have used are MailChimp and Infusionsoft.)

Email marketing allows you to personalise communication, direct people to your website, Facebook page or to other social media sites. You can offer deals or simply provide high-quality content that you believe will benefit the reader.

I am sure you have been on the receiving end of emails that serve only to fill up your inbox. Your challenge is not to be someone who sends emails that are looked upon in this way.

As with any online interaction it needs to be of value to the reader. Even with this, you need to be realistic about the response you will get. Don't be surprised if you get 5% or less of those you contact responding to the emails in the way you wish.

Another very important requirement of email campaigns is ensuring your emails are not considered to be spam. If those receiving your emails report them as spam in their email account you could be blocked from sending further emails to potential customers. If you are using email marketing software for bulk emails they may remove you from their site. Worse still you could be in breach of the law.

In the USA, for example, appropriate use of email communication is covered by the CAN-SPAM Act. There are similar laws in many other countries.

A few key questions to ask when sending emails, to reduce your chances of being considered spam, include:

- Did the recipient of the email give you permission to engage with them?
- Do they know why you are engaging with them?
- Have you authenticated who you are?
- Can the recipient opt out of emails or unsubscribe from further emails (as opposed to reporting you as spam)?
- Is any of the information misleading?

An important point to remember is that spam is defined by the receiver of the email, not by you. You may feel what you are providing is extremely useful and high quality. If the recipient doesn't agree with you, they could report your emails as spam.

So think carefully about what you are sending and whom you are sending it to so you can make the most of your email marketing.

Social media

The growth in social media has been quite extraordinary. The following table gives you a sense of how social media has grown in the last decade.

Social media	Start date	Approximate number of current users*
Facebook	2004	1.2 billion
Twitter	2006	645 million
Google Plus	2011	540 million
LinkedIn	2002	300 million
Instagram	2010	150 million
Pinterest	2010	17 million

*Exact numbers vary slightly, depending on the information source.

There are many social media options you could choose to use to reach your current and potential customers. The table above is only a small set of what is available.

While it is interesting to see the size of each social media platform, how do they differ and which platform should you use? The following explanation of how a donut shop might use each platform may be helpful in deciding which platform may work for you (by the way, I found this explanation on social media).

Logo	Social Media	How it is used
	Twitter	I am eating a #donut
	Facebook	I like donuts
	Instagram	Here is a vintage photo of my donut
	YouTube	Watch me eat a donut
	LinkedIn	My skills include eating a donut
	Pinterest	Here is a donut recipe

Social media is changing continually. It was once solely used for personal communication. Now, it is a major place to do business.

Surveys produced by the online marketing firm Vertical Response found that small businesses are increasing their use of social media. Small businesses are spending more time on social media and are showing an increased willingness to pay for that presence. However, small businesses, not surprisingly, struggle with the added workload associated with a strong social media presence.

Many small businesses choose social media as their only source of online marketing. A key consideration with this is determining how much freedom and control you want over your online presence. Remember, if you use a social media platform, the site dictates what you can and can't do. If you develop your own website, you have complete ownership as well as the freedom to manage how you interface with your customers and how you are viewed.

Many small businesses use both, with each medium being a means to link to the other. If you have the resources to do this, having both a website and a social media presence is far more powerful than one alone.

If you are aiming to market through a social media site, the core marketing principles remain. Firstly, you need to know your customers. This will influence which social media site you favour and how you use it. As with any online content, make sure it adds value to your customers and raises their view of your competence and trustworthiness.

You also need to be clear of your resource capabilities. If you have a large presence on a number of social media sites, it could take you significant time to keep these sites up to date and relevant. If you don't have the time, you will need to consider the cost of using a social media service provider in your budget.

I believe you should choose the social media that best meets your customers' needs. If this can be achieved through a number of sites, choose the site (or sites) you are most familiar with and enjoy being on the most.

As with all your marketing efforts, review what is working and what isn't, and be prepared to change course.

Blogs

Blogs (short for 'web logs') are another low-cost means of sharing valuable content online. They are also an excellent place to get views from other business owners in similar situations to you.

You can provide blogs through a huge range of small business forums. Social media sites like LinkedIn allow you to enter blog discussions with like-minded people through a number of specific groups. There are many websites and blog sites devoted to small business.

A few of the more popular business blog sites include:

- Ezine Articles
- AllBusiness
- Neil Patel of Quick Sprout

- Small Business Trends
- Seth Godin
- LinkedIn groups
- SlideShare.

As with social media, blogs should be a way of providing useful content to potential or existing customers who in turn are directed to your website.

If you offer good quality information in your blogs, especially if they trigger discussions or debate, it will raise people's awareness of you. It may not necessarily lead directly to more customers, but it will increase people's awareness of you, will lift your credibility with peers and may lead to referrals.

Online advertising

There are a number of different methods you can use to advertise your business online. The principles for online marketing are no different to any other. Know who your customer is and choose the medium most likely to reach them. If they are heavy internet users, including social media, then online advertising could be a very effective method.

People using the internet are used to getting a wealth of material for little or no cost. If your advertising is solely selling you or your products, it is likely to attract less interest. To get a user to click on your advertisement and get redirected to your website, you need to offer them something to make it worth their while.

Common online advertising media are Google AdWords and advertisements on popular social media sites such as LinkedIn and Facebook, which allow you to manage your budget.

Google AdWords are the entries at the top of a Google search (marked with 'Ad' beside the text). Getting to the top of these searches involves good keyword use and may involve higher bid prices. The methods to manage your online advertising budget include:

- **Pay-per-click.** In pay-per-click, you only pay when a person clicks on the advertisement. Whether they do anything after being directed from the advertisement doesn't matter. You still pay for the click. The price you pay per click will vary depending on what you are trying to advertise. Very general and popular topics will require much higher bid prices to get the priority. Less popular could be a few cents to a few dollars per click. This is a good way of ensuring you only pay if someone is interested enough to take action towards getting what you're offering. How they act will depend a lot on the quality of the offer.
- **Pay-per-1000-impressions.** In this method, you pay a set cost for each 1000 times your advertisement is viewed when a webpage is opened, no matter how many clicks you receive. This is a good option if you care more about the number of times your ad is shown than getting clicks.

The other advantage of this type of advertising is your ability to tailor the campaign to target particular audiences.

LinkedIn has the ability for you to be very specific who and where you target. It could be by industry, job title, employer, skills and so on. This is much more effective than a newspaper advertisement or billboard.

Likewise, Google AdWords will only bring up the advertisement for those searching for what you are offering. They also allow detailed analytics on the interest you have generated. This allows you to amend the campaign as you go.

If you have a website, this is another way of effectively finding the 'tourists in the Amazon jungle' and directing them to the 'sign' you want them to see, namely your website.

Analyse what worked through customer feedback

No matter what methods you use to market your small business, you need to consider how you track what has worked. With traditional marketing, you may have to ask customers when they first engage with you how they found you — newspapers, paper drops, radio and so on.

It is also worth finding some simple ways to get feedback from customers about how good your product or service was and what you could do to improve it. This could be through online survey methods (like Survey Monkey), through an independent person, or simply by talking directly with your clients.

Summary

Let's pull some of the key points together from the above discussion so that you can develop a simple plan for your marketing.

- Remain clear on your business's purpose, values, and goals and ensure your marketing aligns to deliver this.
- Think carefully about what your business's products or services add to people's lives. Who is most likely to benefit from what you do?
- Know the clear difference between what you offer and what your competitors do. This is your point of difference. If you don't know what it is, no-one else will.
- Write down your point of difference. Make sure you can describe it in 20–30 seconds.
- Know your competitors and what makes you different from them.
- Define who your ideal customers are at this stage in your business's life.
- Write down the key pieces of information about those customers.
- List the best ways you feel you can reach these customers (radio, magazines, flyers, social media, web searches, networking groups, sports or social events, schools, universities, business associations, etc.).
- Recheck pricing against your competitors, including all costs and margins.

- List the different media you could use to maximise your connections with current and new customers. Start with the most effective to least effective.
- Make the final decision based on what you can afford.
- Consider what your online presence is and what it should be.

After working through all these points, throw as much as you can down and start piecing together a marketing plan for the next 12 months.

Finally:

- Consider the methods by which you'll establish what marketing initiatives worked and those that didn't (remembering that online marketing is by far the easiest to track).
- Be prepared to fail quickly and fail cheaply. Then move on if one option produces nothing, ensuring of course that you're not being too impatient (especially online). If you see something 'failing', don't lose the idea altogether, as it may work at some future date or in a different medium.
- Remember, the most trusted and effective marketing for any-sized business is receiving a referral from a reliable person. This is also the lowest-cost marketing. A positive word from a satisfied customer is free. Once you earn the right to serve a customer, do it really well.

Questions

- Who are your ideal customers?
- What characteristics would you use to describe your ideal customers?
- How would you describe your brand?
- What is the point of difference between your business and your competitors' businesses?
- What benefits will your products or services bring to people's lives?
- How confident are you that you are pricing correctly?
- What are you doing to promote your business?
- How effective is your promotion in generating new customers?
- How many referrals are you getting from satisfied customers?
- What are you doing online to promote your business?

Chapter 9
How to Employ and Keep
the Best People

As the statistics discussed earlier indicate, most of us in business are solos who don't employ people. In fact, many of us avoid it for a whole range of reasons.

It's unlikely that anyone you employ will have the passion for your business that you do. You may find the concept of managing people to be hard work. Employees can also become a high cost for you and you may feel responsible for your employees' financial future as well as your own. This could constitute an unnecessary stress that you just don't need.

Our fear to employ can be a major stumbling block to our growth or even our survival. Our success, especially in service-based industries, is often limited by the number of hours we can work. To make more money, we work harder and longer. Employing the right staff and then looking after them, in a way that gets the most out of them, is critical.

Remember the 'human' in human resources

After many years of managing staff, I've often seen the profession that is Human Resources forget the most critical part of what it is meant to do: look after the people. It's an area of many businesses that can get overrun with the pressures of process. Recruitment, equal opportunity, remuneration, performance management and payroll are examples of processes that are required in any business when staff are employed, including in small businesses.

It is so important that you don't lose sight of the most important fact about your new staff. They are people with their own weaknesses, strengths, goals and desires. They will have their own life issues. They could bring these issues from home to work. They are likely to have a different temperament to you. They'll have different personalities. Different situations will stress them. Their diversity could be a huge asset or a huge headache.

While you must be conscious of following the right processes, don't get swamped in them at the expense of treating your staff as human beings.

You must select the right people, manage your expectations of them, and not accept unacceptable behaviours. If you do get the right person through the door, look after that employee. Treat him or her with respect. Show empathy and care for your staff. Remember your values. Your staff will scrutinise your behaviours more than anyone. Keep front of mind that you are human too. You don't have to know everything and you will make mistakes. Admit this to your staff, as they will respect you for it. Most of all, be yourself. Having other people working beside you and sharing in your business can be hugely rewarding.

Short-term options to find staff

Let's get into some of the mechanics of bringing people into your business.

We've discussed the wide range of external experts you can engage to help you when necessary. The good thing about using people in this way is it's a short-term cost where you can pursue the exact skill you want at the time you need it. You can also stop it when you don't need or can no longer afford it.

You may well require support over a longer period but only for a limited number of hours each month. For example, you may wish to get someone to manage your accounts at the end of the month. This might take a day each month for a qualified person. Rather than employ a full-time administration person, you may engage a service provider who can do this for you. They may charge a higher hourly rate but you don't have any of the work that comes with employing someone.

These types of short-term relationships are always easier to end than they are for permanent employees, including if things are not working out.

Full-time employees

If you're growing, you will need to look seriously at employing full-time staff.

There are many advantages of full-time staff over short-term options:

- They're usually far more committed to the long term.
- You don't have to continually retrain people.
- You have the opportunity to build a strong, lasting relationship.
- They should provide greater continuity for customers.
- They allow you to delegate your tasks.
- They also provide possible successors.

If the growth is strong, you may need to employ a number of people in a very short space of time. Even if your need for staff becomes urgent, employing the wrong people in a very small business can cause major issues (and stress). There are some key processes you should follow to reduce the chances of these challenging situations arising.

Often, small businesses put too little time into employing the right people. Many owners struggle to manage their employees or simply dislike the challenges of people management and possible conflicts.

Many owners are petrified of the legal aspects of the employment process and tolerate poor performance. They fear that action may lead to formal grievances, legal issues, unwanted costs and distractions from their business.

Owners can struggle to understand why their employees are not as devoted to the business as they are, and build unrealistic expectations. Many don't articulate what they expect of their employees, give them useful feedback, or assess their performance frequently enough.

While there are no guarantees with people management, some key principles will minimise the pain of getting it wrong.

Selection and recruitment processes

The first and most critical step is recruiting the right people. Small business owners often spend very little time on the recruitment process when it's one of the most important business decisions they have to make.

You may approach someone you know and give them a tap on the shoulder. If no-one comes to mind, you might have to recruit externally.

Before you put an advertisement online or in the local newspaper, form a very clear view of what you want in the person.

- How clear are you on the details of the role you want to fill?
- What are you able to pay and is it enough to attract candidates? Remember that you will be unlikely to compete with large company salaries.
- What, other than salary, makes working with you attractive?
- Define the critical aspects that the candidate needs to demonstrate. As a minimum they need to be aligned with your values.
- What minimum skills must they have?

It is strongly advised that you write up a **job description** for the role, whether you are recruiting a stranger or someone you know. This will help clarify what you want in the role and the person who finally fills it. Further, it will clarify the position for candidates.

The job description should cover the following as a minimum:

- Job title
- Pay range

- Key accountabilities
- Minimum requisite qualifications
- Any financial delegations (what the person can spend without asking your permission)
- Any personal attributes that the person in the role must demonstrate.

The job description is not meant to cover every task. It should be more high level.

There are a number of methods you can use to reach out to potential candidates. The type of person you are seeking will influence how you advertise. Consider the possible candidates and, just like customers, think about how best to engage them. Local newspapers, trade magazines and online recruitment websites are common. Social media sites are becoming particularly popular too.

How much of the recruitment process you complete yourself and how much you outsource to a recruitment business will depend on the time, skill and your funding. For more senior or difficult roles, a recruitment company may be a good investment. You should shop around to find the best recruiter for you. If you find a recruitment company you are happy with, they can become a very beneficial advisor for your business should you grow.

If you have the option, interview two or three candidates. It helps if you have another person with you to get a broader perspective and to avoid subconscious biases. When asking questions, get the candidates to offer specific examples where they demonstrated the skills and behaviours you are looking for. An example question might be, "Tell me about a time you had a disagreement with a fellow employee or boss and how you resolved it."

Always ask for references and follow up on them. Don't rely on written references, as they could have been written by anyone. Speak directly to referees. If candidates can't provide references, you should ask them why not, as it could raise some suspicion. While candidates will normally only give you references that are likely to be positive, it is surprising what you can discover if you ask referees some probing questions.

Depending on the role, you may also wish to do additional checks on the individual. This could include their criminal history, driving status (especially if driving is essential for the job they will be doing), and even credit-worthiness. It is very likely you will need to gain the applicant's permission to do these checks. If so, include these details in the application.

I would caution you against recruiting close friends or family unless you are both very clear on the needs of the business and the relationship. There are many cases of businesses that have successfully operated with family and friends involved, but just as many where long-standing relationships have been seriously damaged by the pressures of small business. Don't just do it because it's a convenient option. Do it because the person is right for your business.

☞ *If the candidates are not right for you, don't employ anyone. Start looking again. While you may feel pain to remain under-resourced and frustrated with the time and cost to recruit, the pain you will feel if you employ the wrong person could be infinitely worse.*

Set clear expectations from day one

The clearer you can make your expectations known to the new employee, the better. It could remove a lot of heartache at a later date.

These could be very high-level expectations or quite detailed. How detailed may depend on the balancing act between sufficient clarity and scaring off a potential employee after being overrun with what they may see as petty rules.

Here are a few examples:

- A café owner makes it clear to new employees that staff cannot take food for free, but are welcome to buy food at cost price.
- An electrician tells new staff they must be at the office every morning at 7 a.m. for a safety and planning meeting.
- A new receptionist is told how to answer all phone calls to support even the most difficult customer.

You should reinforce your business values and how important they are to you. You may find an employee meets the requirements of their job description but behaves in a way that is at odds with the values you hold dear.

The job descriptions you prepared for the recruitment process should be finalised and signed by you and the new employee. This document may not detail everything the person does, but it is a critical document especially if you or the employee disputes the requirements of the role.

Typically, a **contract of employment** is a legal requirement. Ensure that the candidate is fully aware of their requirements under the contract. Employment law that applies to you may differ from place to place. If you have no experience in completing a contract of employment, it's highly important to seek the right advice. There are processes that government agencies give small business owners to complete these documents and some industry advocacy groups offer it for members. Human resource advisory companies and employment lawyers also provide this service and will be better at tailoring a specific contract that meets both the law and your specific needs. Normally, you will only need to do this once, as the contract of employment should only require minor changes for any additional employees.

Avoid the temptation to get new staff started before all the paperwork has been signed. This seems like an obvious thing but I know far too many businesses that are so pleased to get the right person they start them as soon as possible, saying they will sort out the paperwork later . . . and never do.

Manage and support your staff's performance

One of the things most small business owners dislike is disciplining an employee when they are not meeting expectations. Unfortunately, it is something you can't avoid. It is vitally important you monitor and manage your staff's performance. This includes addressing poor performance and also acknowledging the good things they are doing.

I'm often asked by business owners what they should do if they see substandard performance. The one thing you should never do is 'nothing'. The specific actions you take will depend heavily on your style and approach to staff, your relationship with the person, the person's possible responses and the specifics of the issue.

If the performance issue is minor and just a one-off, you may make a note in case you see it again. If it happens more often, your response could be as simple as a quiet word reminding the person of your expectations. If the issues continue, or worsen, you may need to increase the action required. It's very important to document every stage of this process. It could become vital information if the situation worsens to the point where you may have to let the person go.

If dismissal is starting to look like your only option, it is highly critical that you seek advice, especially if you have no prior experience. If you react prematurely and get this process wrong, it could cost you a lot in legal fees to defend your decision. Not to mention the significant stress and reduced time for your business.

There are likely to be many employment law cases in your jurisdiction, stemming from dismissals, which have produced decisions you consider unfair to a business owner. This is further reason to seek advice rather than resorting to what you think makes sense from your perspective.

The counter to poor performance is how you acknowledge good performance. Business owners can often get so tied up in the day-to-day challenges of the business that they don't stop and simply say, "Thank you, that was great" and "I really appreciate what you did." It can make a huge difference to an employee. This type of reward can often be more powerful than any financial or other material reward.

Hone your management and leadership skills

When you finally reach the time to employ people you can look upon it with dread or take it on with a positive mindset. Being a solo can be lonely. It's exciting to share your successes with someone else and uplifting to have someone there if you fail. It gives you the chance to build the leadership and management skills you probably have always had but never needed to use.

Here are a few tips for being a better small business leader:

- Remember that your employee is a whole person who has a life outside work. Be prepared to engage with the whole person and learn about them.

- Consider this statement about leadership: 'Know yourself; accept yourself; forget yourself.' Leadership is often about being selfless. Putting your staff and your business before you will build loyalty. You will receive rewards in other ways.
- Be prepared to delegate responsibilities to your staff. This may require your guidance, mentoring and oversight, depending on the staff's experience.
- You cannot lead others if you are unable to know and lead yourself. Revisit the work you did on yourself in the earlier chapters. Having clarity on your strengths and weaknesses will make you a better leader. You won't be expected to know everything. Remember that you, like every leader, are human.
- Stand by your staff and they will back you. They will make mistakes. Human error is normal. The key is that they learn from them. If they don't and it starts hurting your business, pursue this with them.
- Communicate often with your staff. People tend to fill in the gaps when there is a lack of information and it's usually filled with unproductive or incorrect information.

> *"Trust but verify."*
>
> *"Surround yourself with the best people you can find, delegate authority, and don't interfere as long as the policy you've decided upon is being carried out."*
> — **Ronald Reagan, former US President**

Summary

Some final thoughts on employing, managing and keeping good people:

- Bringing people into your small business has its risks and challenges. You may be unable to avoid recruiting if you are to achieve your goal.
- Remember, you are employing people. While all the laws, rules and processes are important, the most critical thing to remember is that they are human. They too face all the challenges of being human that we discussed in the early chapters of this book.
- They may not have the passion you have for your business, but they can still offer you a great deal.
- Take some time defining the role you want and spend time recruiting the best person you can.
- Set your expectations as clearly and as early as you can.
- When you see excellent performance or sub-standard performance, never do 'nothing'. A quiet positive word or gentle reminder may help a person know they're appreciated or sort out a bad habit before it gets out of hand.
- If things deteriorate and a person is damaging your business, you have to act. Seek advice, follow good process and have good documentation.

- If you are new to management, you may have much to learn. Be yourself. Be authentic. You are not infallible. Talk to your staff often. You could develop invaluable and truly rewarding relationships with these people.

Questions

- How would you define your leadership and management style?
- How comfortable are you to employ staff?
- How well are you able to define the roles you wish to fill?
- How do you recruit the best candidates?
- How comfortable are you to discuss the performance of your team with them?

Chapter 10
Identifying the Legal Issues for Your Business

A critical issue for any business is abiding by the law. Ignorance of the law has never been, and never will be, an excuse. Neither will the excuse that you're 'too small' and don't have the money or resources to meet all these laws be sufficient. While you may attract some sympathy on this point, it won't serve you at all well in the end if you do breach the law.

It is impossible for me to detail the laws that will apply to your business in this book (I doubt any book can). They will vary greatly in different industries, cities, towns, councils, shires, states and countries.

These laws can cover any, all or even more than the following list:

- Workplace health and safety laws
- Privacy laws
- Consumer protection laws
- Environmental protection
- Anti-trust and anti-competitive behaviour
- Traffic and road use laws
- Employment and labour laws and industrial relations laws
- Online business laws
- Contracts law
- Regulations and laws covering the competency standards for trades and

professionals
- Securities laws
- Bankruptcy laws
- Company law
- Intellectual property laws.

And on it will go. At the most basic level, if your values mean you are always acting with complete honesty, truthfulness, authenticity and ethics, it's a great start towards meeting most legal requirements. However, you do need to know far more about the specifics of your business, the industry and the laws of your jurisdiction to be sure of this.

Some laws require no interpretation. For example, if you exceed the speed limit and are caught, you will be fined. Other laws are far more subjective. For example, as an employer, you need to provide a 'safe and healthy' workplace for your employees and the public. But what constitutes safe?

Can I afford legal support?

As a small business, you won't be able to match the sort of funds that larger businesses can access to put towards legal costs. This does not mean you are unable to gain a better knowledge of what laws apply to you. There are many government-based agencies that offer free online support to at least get you started.

Some examples include:

- New Zealand Companies Office (http://www.business.govt.nz/companies).
- Australian Small Business Commissioner (http://www.asbc.gov.au)
- The US Small Business Administration (www.sba.gov)
- Small Business UK (www.smallbusiness.co.uk)
- The Federation of Small Businesses (www.fsb.org.uk)

There are many more besides and Google is a great place to start researching. Also, if you're a member of the numerous industry advocacy and support groups covering your business area, they normally have legal support available. Often it's even free.

If you are able to narrow in on the legislation, regulations and codes of practice that apply to you and put you at greatest risk, you will be able to drill down further and call on specific help.

Some specific legal areas for small businesses to understand

I have already mentioned the variety of legal contracts and agreements you need to put in place for buying or selling a business, purchasing a franchise, or setting up a partnership, as well as documents required when employing staff.

I will now cover a few specific areas of the law that I believe apply to most small businesses.

Employment Law

We discussed how you can attract and get the most from your staff. As an employer, you will have legal obligations you must fulfil when employing staff. If you are unsure what they are seek good advice. If you get these wrong you may lose a valuable staff member or if it ends in a dispute it could cost you money, time and a lot of emotional energy.

The things you should consider include:

- Minimum rates of pay that must be met
- Minimum leave requirements
- Holidays that are considered statutory and what you must pay staff if you ask them to work.
- Any minimum superannuation requirements
- Ensuring the appropriate employment agreement is in place and adheres to the law.

We also touched on the need for you to act if a staff member is not performing. Allowing poor performance to go unchecked will condone the behaviour which could severely damage your small business. If you find the only outcome is dismissing the staff member be sure you understand the process that is required:

- Have you previously informed the employee of the performance issues?
- Have you sought an explanation?
- Have you given the employee a chance to correct the issue?
- Have you kept good record of all discussions?
- If you are looking to dismiss an employee, have you warned them, in writing, that that is a likely outcome.

Many small business owners are very uneasy about following this process especially if they have not done it before. There is no denying it — its really unpleasant. However, if you don't deal with it the consequences to you and the business could be very serious. Small business owners fear the individual will take legal action against you especially if they feel the process for dismissing them was not followed correctly. No matter how good your process is, a dismissed employee has a right, and may well take a grievance against you. If this does happen seek advice. Resolution of the issue may take time and may even cost some money in the form of legal fees or compensation to the employee. However, this risk is worth taking if the employee staying could damage your business.

Health and Safety

If you have employees or you have customers or community members coming onto your premise you have an obligation to keep them safe from harm. The emotional and legal ramifications if an employee, or customer is seriously injured or killed while at your work place may be extremely serious.

While this may seem a very unlikely scenario for many business owners people are being seriously injured or dying while at work far too regularly.

There are some excellent processes and systems small business owners can follow and support that will assist in making your workplace safer. A few things to consider:

- Staff will take health and safety seriously only if you take it seriously.
- Identify and understand the hazards in the workplace that could cause harm to people.
- If these hazards can be removed, do so. If they can't put processes in place to reduce the chance of them causing harm.
- Talk about safety. Make it a normal part of daily work life.
- Know the regulations and rules that apply to your workplace — seek help if you need to clarify your obligations.
- Try and find the most practical way to meet your obligations and to make the workplace safe.
- Excessive paperwork may not be the best outcome — if you make safety too hard people will bypass it.

While there are many physical and procedural processes that any workplace can put in place to make it safer nothing will keep people safer more than the commitment, attitudes and behaviours of you and your staff.

Intellectual property

In starting a new business or developing new products or services, you may need to consider what unique value they may have and whether you need to protect this value. For many of the largest businesses in the world, it is these assets that hold the greatest value and they defend it vigorously.

Here are a few examples of what *Forbes* magazine lists as some of the most valuable trademarks:

- **Google:** Trademark value $US 44.3 billion (this is 27% of the firm's overall value)
- **Microsoft:** Trademark value $US 42.8 billion (21%)
- **Walmart:** Trademark value $US 36.2 billion (19%)
- **Vodafone:** Trademark value $US 30.7 billion (22%)
- **Apple:** Trademark value $US 25.9 billion (10%).

What is intellectual property?

Nothing about intellectual property (IP) is remotely simple. Even finding a consistent simple definition is no easy task. Despite this, I've endeavoured to provide you one of the better ones:

Intellectual property refers to creations of the mind, such as inventions; literary and artistic works; designs; and symbols, names and images used in commerce.

The process of protecting your unique creations may not be simple and can be expensive. The more you want to protect, and the more countries and regions you want protection in, the more the process will cost you.

The most common types of IP that you are likely to come across are:

- Copyright
- Website domains and company names
- Patents and designs
- Trademarks.

This is a specialised legal area and you should strongly consider specialist legal support to do a full search and to apply for IP protection. You can do a lot of initial investigation on the IP protection you are considering. Places to start your search include:

- The New Zealand Intellectual Property Office (www.iponz.govt.nz)
- IP Australia (www.ipaustralia.gov.au)
- The US Patent and Trademark Office (www.uspto.gov)
- The EU Copyright Office (www.eucopyright.com)
- The US copyright office (www.copyright.gov).

It is not my intention to explain the process (or processes) you will need to follow to protect your IP. However, I raise the issues here so you can consider if there is genuine benefit in considering whether your IP has value and should be protected. At least then you will know when to ask the questions. There are also some simple low-cost actions you can take in some areas that I will touch on.

Copyright

Copyright protects your creative ideas that are expressed in forms such as songs, artwork, drawings, paintings, writing, sculptures, films, software, architecture, websites, graphics, and video games. Copyright does not protect the idea, only the manner in which these ideas are expressed. In short, you have to translate the idea into something real.

In almost every country, your work has automatic copyright protection without you having to take any formal action to protect it. Once it is in a tangible form, it is protected. This protection lasts while you are alive and typically many decades after your death. You should add the symbol © with your company name on all documents you want to protect. While your rights are already reserved, many people still choose to reinforce this by adding the statement 'All rights reserved' even though they don't need to.

You can choose to register the copyright with the appropriate copyright agency in your country. The reason there is benefit in registering the copyright is so your work is on the public record as being protected. It also gives you much greater legal standing if you discover someone has stolen your works and you wish to take action.

What did Michelle decide?

Michelle provides instructions with her products and information on brochures. She wants to remind people that she has automatic copyright over this material and is determined to protect it by adding the following at the bottom of every document:

© Copyright 2014 — Michelle's Organics Company — All Rights Reserved

Michelle decided not to pursue formal registration of the copyright, as the cost was too high at this stage, and the risk to the business quite low. She felt the automatic protection was sufficient.

Trademarks

Trademarks are those names, distinctive words, phrases, graphic designs, slogans or logos that distinguish your products and services from anyone else's. Your logos, product names and company identifiers are a key part of your brand. As such, you need to ensure they are distinctive from any competitors' and you need to consider if there is value in legally protecting them.

Unlike copyright, trademarks are not automatically protected.

You need to establish what value you will gain from protecting your logo, your brand name or your company. Many businesses have operated for many years with distinctive logos that were never registered as a trademark. Your choice to register may also depend on your long-term goal. If you are considering growth and want to use your distinctive brand as part of your strategy, you should consider registration.

While you may choose a trademark in the form of words or images and choose not to register it, you should still be cautious that someone else has not already registered something similar. It will not be good for your business after months of operation, when you are finally getting some exposure, to receive a letter from an IP lawyer saying your image or words conflict with another company who intend to take action if you don't remove it.

As a minimum, you should search the trademark office websites in the country where you want to use the trademark to see if any potential conflicts exist. An experienced IP lawyer will do a more thorough search and advise, if an issue does come up, what the risks might be.

If you have something you want to protect, as a minimum you can use the ™ symbol. This indicates to the world that you are claiming ownership of it. You could do this from the time your trademark is released into the market while you are going through the registration process. Once formally registered, you can add the symbol ®. You cannot use this symbol unless the trademark is registered. The font, style and colours you submit for registration will be the exact details of what is registered. If you want to protect variations to the main trademark, you will need to register them as well.

You will also need to consider the classification applicable to your particular product or service. For example, there are more than 40 international classes listed in the US Patent and Trademark Office (USPTO) trademark process. Therefore, there can be two identical trademarks registered in different classifications in the same country. Trademarking only gives you protection in the country where you have registered and only in the classes you have selected.

Website domains and company names

Your online presence will indicate a lot about you and your brand. Your choice of keywords, domain names, and company details can assist in being found online.

Consider the role of your domain (www.<*your company name*>.com) and registered company names (<*Your Company Name*> Ltd.) as part of your IP. You also need to consider any potential conflicts between domain, company and trademarks.

If you have or intend to build a website, you will need to choose a unique domain name. (Take a look at www.domainname.com.) While no-one will be able to take the domain name off you for their website, you still need to ensure it does not breach someone else's trademark.

Likewise, you may have registered your Limited Liability Company name with your local companies office. Once you have done this, no other company can register this name. However, it remains possible that the company name you chose breaches another party's trademark and they may have a right to challenge you.

For example, Amazon has registered both its company name 'Amazon' and its domain

Michelle's View on Trademarks

Michelle feels that trademark protection is beyond her reach at present, but she still wants to choose a phrase that represents her products. She decides on the following line that she hopes to add to every one of her products:

'A Totally Organic Experience'

She feels this reflects what all her products deliver. In her own country where she wants to use this statement, she finds Procter & Gamble have a registered trademark for this exact phrase in the class 'Hair Care Preparations including Shampoos'. As she has products in mind that will fall into this class, she decides against using a trademark that is registered to another party, especially one of the size of Procter & Gamble. She decides to choose another tagline.

name 'Amazon.com' as trademarks in the US. In short, before settling on a unique domain name, company name, logo or slogan, it is worth doing some searching to see if you could be at odds with an existing company's trademarks.

Secure domain names as soon as you have settled on them even if you don't intend to build a website. It is relatively cheap and you have it for future use.

Patent and designs

A patent is a legal right granted to the patent owner giving them the exclusive rights, for a limited period, to use and develop an invention. Not all 'inventions' are patentable. They need to be novel and useful in an industry. The invention cannot already be known and in use where the patent application is being made.

It is very important that you do not disclose an invention you wish to patent. Once it is in the public domain, been described or used, you may lose the right to patent it. Even if this were not the case, you may face the risk of the idea being taken before you can register it. Therefore, it is critical that your invention remains confidential until you have protections in place.

There are different types of patents. They typically fall into three categories: Utility Patents, Design Patents, and Patents of a New Plant Species.

Utility patents cover new products, processes, equipment or machinery of some kind.

Design patents are to cover a unique and novel appearance or ornamental design of a product. For example, a drink manufacturer may design a unique type of glass bottle for their drink that identifies their product over the bottles of their competitors. Plant patents relate to unique plant varieties. The substance and term of patents vary from country to country, so you will need to consider this. You should, as a minimum, do a preliminary search to see if your invention has already been patented. You may need to seek the expertise of others to do a more thorough search.

Summary

Here are a few key points to consider about the legal aspects of your small business.

- Find out what laws, regulations or codes of practice expose your small business to the greatest risk.
- The answers are out there. You just need to find the lowest-cost way to get them.
- Ignorance due to your small size or limited funds will never be an excuse for failing to obey the laws. You are just as accountable to the law as the largest corporations.
- Understand the risks and liabilities you face personally from your business activities. Put appropriate processes in place to protect your personal life from your business life.
- You will have legal obligations when you employ staff and if you are faced with dismissing staff.
- Ensure your workplace is safe and you and your staff take safety seriously.
- Your business's greatest value may be in its intellectual property. Consider

copyright, trademark or patent options.

- Protecting your IP can be complex and expensive. Understand what benefits it will bring before committing.
- Be careful that you don't breach other people's intellectual property. It could prove very painful and costly.

Questions

- What laws have the most impact on your business?
- How confident are you that you are meeting your health and safety obligations?
- What intellectual property exists in your business?
- What benefit would be protecting your IP bring the business?

Chapter 11
Systems and Processes for Your Daily Operations

Some simple tips to assist in your day-to-day business life

A day in the life of your business will vary dramatically from other businesses. You know your business better than anyone. You need to be on the lookout for how you can make your day-to-day activities easier and more efficient for you. But it's also prudent to consider what you're doing each day and whether it moves you closer to your goals. The danger is that the busier you get, the less efficient your business could become.

Here are a few tips that may help, in some small way, to improve a day in your business's life:

- **Wasted Time**: Occasionally, keep track in more detail of where you spend your time. If you are service-based, how many hours are you billing and how many hours attract no revenue? Are you wasting too much time doing things that add little value?
- **Keep an eye on the dollars**: By the time you finish this book, you'll be sick of hearing me talk about keeping an eye on your cash. No apologies will be forthcoming on this point. Cash is your lifeblood, so keep an eye on it as often as you can.
- **Remember your personal rules**: When we talked about YOU, I highlighted the need to set a few basic rules to ensure you look after yourself. These will differ for

everyone. Whatever yours are, do your best to stick to them. Any of these ideas could work for you: turn your phone off at 6 p.m.; pick up the kids twice a week; go for your daily walk or run; meet a friend for coffee once a week; do a daily gym session; schedule in meditation, and so on.

- **Inventory**: What's happening with your inventory? If it's rising or falling abnormally, it may give you an early indication of the health of your business.
- **Trend your KPIs**: When you set your key performance indicators in your business plan, consider only those that make a real difference and make them measurable. Keep a regular eye on them, observing how they are trending, whether they are improving or not.
- **Talk to your customers**: They are what will decide your fate. Keep in touch with them in the easiest way you can.
- **Talk to your staff**: Even if there are only a few of you, work at your communication. Catch up regularly so you all know what's going on.
- **Spend time on the business**: Set aside a little time each month to look at the business, rather than only working in the business.
- **Look out for waste**: Anything using materials or time that adds no value to the business or your customers is waste.
- **Keep the place tidy**: If you work in a mess, it is likely your business will be, or will be perceived as, a mess by staff and customers.
- **Plan**: Do some planning, weekly or monthly, to keep you and your small team focused on the priorities.
- **Celebrate your successes**: You may frequently find yourself and your team too busy to reflect on how well you're going. Fit in a small amount of time to celebrate your successes. You deserve it. Enjoy them.

Time — your most precious resource — how to manage it better

The most valuable and precious thing you have and can give to another is your time. Yet as small business owners we may not manage the use of this valuable resource as well as we could.

Just as you have to make choices when deciding your strategy, as we covered in Chapter 4, you must make choices in how you prioritise your time.

Successful time management is about prioritisation. The most important priorities are those that deliver on goals and your core purpose. They may not be those urgent tasks that swamp you every day. You need to consider short-term urgent priorities and also longer-term important priorities.

Once you have an idea of these priorities consider the following list. What resonates most for you?

- **Devote time working ON the business**: It is one of the most overused cliché's for small business owners yet very few actually do it. Set aside time each month to review how your business is going, where it is going and how you are going.
- **Personal wellbeing rules**: If you have decided to include a few rules to improve your wellbeing, like exercise, time with family and friends, make them a high priority.
- **Be decisive**: It is better to make a decision on the best available information you have than to wait until everything is clear and the opportunity is lost.

> *"It is even better to act quickly and err*
> *than to hesitate until the time of action is past."*
> **Karl Von Clausewitz**

- **Don't Procrastinate**: Procrastinating chews up huge amounts of time, increases your stress, and will affect your business. Identify when you are doing it. If it is an unpleasant task that you hold off completing, then it will only be there tomorrow.
- **Avoid Interruptions**: If you need to get important tasks done without interruptions, then dedicate time to complete them away from the distractions.
- **Avoid multi-tasking**: We often hear people boast about being good multi-taskers. Avoid multi-tasking. There is no prize for doing a lot of tasks poorly rather than one task really well.
- **Set deadlines and stick to them**: Learn to set deadlines for tasks and then finish them. Sometimes simply finishing a task, irrespective of its impact, is a reward in itself.
- **Manage your emails**: Emails are one of the easiest methods of communicating in business but can be overwhelming. Take action on each email. Delete them if they add no value. Act on them immediately, whenever you can. Be brief. People don't like long emails so no point writing long emails that won't be read.
- **Write things down**: Some people have a gift to commit things to memory and then recall them. Unfortunately most of us don't, especially if we are experiencing overload. So write those important and urgent things down so you remember them. This could become your to-do list.
- **Use a calendar or weekly planner**: This is important for you and any members of your small team. Calendars can be easily shared so everyone can assess what everyone is doing.
- **Be punctual and expect punctuality**: If you are sloppy getting to appointments it will tell all those around you that time and discipline is not important to you.
- **Social media**: Differentiate what is important time being spent on Facebook or LinkedIn for the business versus the time spent on entertaining gossip – and, therefore, a waste of time.

- **Networking versus social catch-ups**: Networking brings more customers or strengthens partnerships and is important. Likewise, a social catch up may be an important rule for your wellbeing. Know the difference and make sure your networking is helping your business, not wasting your time.
- **Control the controllable**: It is important to stay informed on what is happening in the outside world. However, don't get hung up on external world issues that you cannot control or even influence.
- **Build routine and habits**: The more you get into habits like those above, the easier they will become. The routine and habits on the little things free you up for the important, innovative, and even fun things.
- **Be responsible. Be disciplined**: Once you commit to any or all of the above points, be responsible. and stick with them. If you consider the great performers in any field, it's their attention to detail and discipline over the long term that helped them achieve their success.

Exploring 'lean' processes

Lean manufacturing processes have been around for a long time. They were widely used in the Japanese car industry, particularly Toyota. At its simplest level, lean processes are aimed at finding **waste** in any business of any size and then doing something about eliminating those wasteful practices. Waste is anything that is not adding value to your business. In his book *The Factory of One*, Daniel Markovitz defines something to be 'value-adding' when:

- The customer is willing to pay for the activity
- The activity transforms your product or service, and
- The activity is done correctly the first time.

Your time is so precious; the worst thing you can do is waste that time on things that add no value.

From time to time, if you feel you are spinning your wheels but not heading in a forwards direction, stop and ask what you are doing that is simply wasting your time (and money).

Usually, we are pretty good at eliminating waste. The issue is identifying the waste.

A lean technique called 5S represents a way to consider and manage waste. In Japanese, these are Seiri, Seiton, Seiso, Seiketsu and Shitsuke, which translate in English to Sort, Straighten, Shine, Standardise and Sustain.

In simple terms, find a place for everything and keep it tidy. Clean up your desk, office and workshop. Keep on top of your filing and throw out things that add no value. Manage your emails using Outlook Rules, or other similar email tool, responding to key messages immediately (especially those from customers) and deleting what you don't want.

A little time every now and then looking for waste and removing it could have a huge benefit on the efficiency of your business, not to mention YOUR sanity.

Systems to improve your daily operations

Most small businesses that I come across could use better systems and processes. This is especially the case for businesses with older owners or people who are not very computer literate and reluctant to change historical practices. While plenty of businesses have survived on paper-based systems, it is getting much harder to do this in the current business world.

With the variety and power of small business software packages and apps on the market, there is no reason why your small business cannot access relatively low-cost, high-quality software systems. If chosen well, they can solve many day-to-day issues. There has been an avalanche of software packages and business apps coming onto the market over recent years and this is likely to continue. The discussion on cognitive overload and choice in previous chapters is very relevant here. I see many businesses throw their hands up trying to find the right system and end up doing nothing.

The most valuable systems are those that replace repetitive but necessary actions, collect important business data for decision-making, and remove the need for you to do anything you particularly dislike.

If you already have a solution for managing your day-to-day operations and are happy with it, you may not need to change anything, just because there's a better option out there. However, keep in mind what your future needs might be. Your current system may very quickly surpass its use-by date and it doesn't hurt to be prepared for this.

An all-too-typical story of system issues

To assess your need to change a system or install a new one, as well as choosing something suitable for your small business, let's walk through a scenario that I've found on repeated occasions with various building-based businesses, such as electricians, plumbers, builders:

The business owner bought the small business or started it from nothing. Work was recorded on paper or in very crude online tools. Each new job required a quote or estimate, which was created on paper and posted or handed to the customer. Once the job started, costs were tracked (where possible) against each job on handwritten timesheets, including hours and materials. The owners and their small crews were great tradespeople but very poor with paperwork so records weren't especially consistent or accurate. At the end of each month, the owner would go through the timesheets and create an invoice, which was sent out to each customer.

The operational problems this created included:
- *No ability to track the accuracy of quotes and estimates.*
- *No ability to establish the gross profit on each job to establish which were profitable.*
- *Inconsistency in quoting and estimating.*
- *Very little traceable history on each customer, the work that was provided and future potential work.*

- *Increased accountancy costs at year-end pulling everything together.*
- *Limited ability to track cash flow and total profitability each month.*
- *Wasted time and effort reconciling invoices with prices for materials and labour each month.*
- *Costs were not accurately linked to the right jobs.*
- *Invoices were taking too long to develop, going out too slowly and delaying payments, whereas suppliers were far more efficient in chasing money, putting pressure on cash flow.*

If this is a story to which you can relate, whether you are in a trade industry or not, start looking at a few other systems options. Not only will this type of scenario be hurting your business, but it will start driving you crazy.

Shortlisting small business software options

Here are a few things to consider for shortlisting your options:

1. Establish what operational issues you are trying to solve before you begin looking at solutions.
2. Will a software solution remove mundane repetitive tasks, increase revenue, reduce costs, save you time or reduce stress? If the answer is yes, start looking at options. There is bound to be a solution that meets this need.
3. Ask other people in similar businesses what they use.
4. Ask your accountant or advisor for some input.
5. Spend some time online reading software reviews and blogs.
6. Shortlist no more than three solutions.
7. Check your shortlisted option(s) against your list of issues to ensure they will actually address them.
8. Most software providers will have free trial demos, online videos and a help desk. Use these free options. If the supplier doesn't supply a trial period, drop them off the list.
9. How easy is the software to use? If it is not user-friendly, move on. There is no reason these days to choose systems that are not user-friendly.
10. Make sure you know all the costs, what you get for it and whether the increased costs of this choice can be recovered through increased sales, reduced costs in your business or reduced time for you.
11. Look to systems that have a strong local presence. There may be excellent alternatives, but with little or no local support it could be an issue when you need help. Larger software providers manage this through strong online and phone-based support.
12. Consider what time you will need to learn it, set it up and then use it.
13. If you don't have the skills to set up the system look for people who can help you.

The cost may be well worth it

14. If you are likely to need two or three systems across the business, check whether they can easily integrate and work together. For example, does your payroll system talk to your accounting system? Does inventory information feed into your financial software? Does time sheeting access materials information from inventory?

15. Don't go for a sophisticated system if you don't need it. Avoid jumping at the shiniest new product that comes into sight.

If you find and install the best system for your business, you will wonder how you previously survived without it.

☞ *If I were to recommend one system in which every size of business should invest, it's your* **financial and accounting system***. There are many low-cost options out there, both Cloud and desktop. Every business must receive money, spend money, and pay taxes month in and month out.*

Cloud-based software . . . What is it? Why use it?

The traditional model for business computing for any-sized business was to house all your information on your computer hard drive or server in your home or office. Software was downloaded as a one-off CD purchase either from your local computer shop or from the vendor's network on the internet. If software upgrades occurred, you might have had to purchase new software or pay for upgrades.

To protect your business from a loss of data, you had to back up your hard drive and preferably have that backup drive remote from your main hard drive (in case of fire or theft, for example). If you were away from the server or hard drive, you were limited in the information you could access. If there was more than one user, you might have to buy additional licences and put them on additional computers, unless you were networked. There was no ability to access any of this information from your smartphone or tablet.

Not any more.

All that has changed and 'Cloud' computing offers another option. The Cloud is not some mythical place where data floats around freely for all the world to see. Simply put, rather than data being stored and managed on your hard drive, it is stored and managed on huge servers in locations around the world. You can access the Cloud anywhere and with any device that can access the internet.

Benefits of Cloud-based computing

Here are some reasons why Cloud-based software is proving so popular.

■ **Competition in small business Cloud computing**
Many Cloud-based suppliers are targeting small businesses. They too are aware of

how many of us exist. The growth of Cloud-based software has made high-quality, user-friendly software available to small businesses at an achievable price.

- ■ **Security**
  Security is improved, as it is not reliant on the hard drive of a single machine.

- ■ **Remote access**
  You can log into your Cloud-based systems wherever you have access to the internet. This includes your smartphone and tablet. You can also give permission to third parties (e.g. your accountant, your bank or other financial support people) to access your systems remotely. This allows them to do most of their work without accessing your hard drive or relying on you transferring documents from your hard drive to them.

- ■ **Choice and flexibility**
  The Cloud has opened a huge array of new Cloud software, apps and mobile device features that add greater flexibility to your business. These include credit card payments from your phone; photographing and processing receipts; onsite, on-the-spot quotes on your tablet; links to Google Maps to direct you to a customer's location via GPS tracking, and so on. Also, there is nothing to say if you buy one Cloud-based option that you can't continue to use other existing desktop options. It's not an all-or-nothing switch.

- ■ **Easier communication between Cloud packages**
  Many Cloud-based business solutions are designed to seamlessly talk to other online systems. For example, your payroll system can dump labour costs into the accounting system. The accounting system can drag stock levels and pricing data from the inventory system.

Possible issues with Cloud-based computing

- ■ **Assumption that your data is fully backed-up in the Cloud**
  While the information is stored remotely, it does not guarantee it is backed up. If you delete something at your PC, it is deleted in the Cloud. If a document is corrupted on your PC, it is corrupted in the Cloud. If you want genuine backup, you may need to opt for one of the many backup offers that are also Cloud-based.

- ■ **Cost**
  Many feel choosing to go with a Cloud option may be cheaper. It often isn't. You may pay hundreds (or thousands) of dollars for new desktop software. The equivalent Cloud-based software may only cost $US 20–50/month. However, it won't take long for the cost of the Cloud option to exceed the desktop option overall. There is also a trap that you buy a Cloud-based package and find you are adding a range of add-ons to get the full flexibility you need. Monthly charges can really grow doing this.

As with any decision, you should weigh up the costs versus the benefits of all the choices available.

So what did the tradespeople in our examples choose?

While I won't go through the specific systems and suppliers that the tradespeople chose in my case study, I'll summarise the various systems that improved efficiency of operations for a few. The software systems they chose are in wide use, are very cost-effective, and all the owners now wonder why they didn't use them before. These included:

- Cloud-based small business accounting software.
- A job management system that each tradesperson could use to enter time and materials via their mobile device.
- GPS tracking through the job management system, so each tradesman could go straight to the correct jobsite with details of the job on hand.
- A simple customer relationship management (CRM) system that allowed the owner to keep track of all past, existing and potential new customers, and all their details.
- A simple app that could scan receipts using a smartphone and automatically enter the data into the accounting software.
- A system provided by the bank, allowing credit card payments, through a smartphone, directly to the business bank account. The Cloud-based accounting system then picks up this information.
- A payroll system that collected all hours from the smartphone entries of each tradesman, in the job management system, organised their pay, and automatically paid their taxes.
- An inventory management system that kept track of everything the tradesman used, kept up-to-date inventory levels and assisted with reordering when stock levels dropped.

These systems brought huge benefit to the businesses that installed them.

Summary

Here are the key points in managing the day-to-day running of your small business:

- Following some basic disciplines to do the little things right will show through in the speed, cost and quality of the product and services you provide.
- Look out for those things that take up your time or money, but add no value to your customers or business. A small amount of time doing this could save a lot of money and effort in the long run.
- Before looking at a software solution, understand your problems and then look at what options will address them.
- If your processes are not up to scratch, do something. Small businesses of all sizes are spoilt for choice with the software options now on the market.
- You have no excuse to have poor systems in your small business. The rapid growth in high-quality, relatively inexpensive Cloud-based software continues and much of

this growth is targeted at small business.

- The biggest issue is filtering through the noise to find the right option. Know the issue you want to solve. Do some searching for the solutions to address these problems. Ask around. Spend some time online. Then choose.

Questions

- What will you do to improve the management of your time?
- How could you improve the day-to-day running of your business?
- What systems do you need to improve?
- What software systems might help the running of your business?

Chapter 12

So . . . How's Your Bottom Line? Understanding and Managing the Finances

The *Oxford English Dictionary* defines the general term 'The Bottom Line' as:

The fundamental and most important factor.

In a business's financial statements, the bottom line is usually considered to be the final number that pops out of the business. Typically, that is the profit after everything has been paid.

If you consider both the financial and the general meanings of this phrase, you would probably think that profit is the most important factor in your business and, as such, should be where all your attention is focused.

I put a slightly different slant on the meaning of 'The Bottom Line' in your business:

The bottom line comes by paying attention to everything above that line.

Don't get me wrong. If you're a commercial business, you are there to make money. And the more money you can make, the better. However, don't get blinded by an unhealthy focus on that line. Don't forget that what pops out at the bottom is determined by everything else you do above the line and what's been done beforehand.

If you have paid really good attention to all the previous chapters, the bottom line should look after itself.

Many small business owners dislike bookkeeping. Unless you are a closet accountant, I am quite sure you didn't get into your business to look at the financials all day long.

Whether you like it or not, though, you must understand the accounts to a reasonable level and you can't hand it all over to someone else and hope for the best. Tracking financial performance is all too often done poorly.

I have also come across many business owners who feel intimidated by the financials and sit with their accountant fearful to ask what may seem like a dumb question.

Remember, if you don't ask questions, you won't understand. If you don't understand your business, who else can you expect to understand it?

> *"There are naive questions, tedious questions, ill-phrased questions, questions put after inadequate self-criticism. But every question is a cry to understand the world. There is no such thing as a dumb question."*
> — **Carl Sagan, author and scientist**

Please, ask and ask again!

This chapter aims to give you enough information to understand the financial aspects of your business. It's not going to teach you how to prepare your annual accounts or allow you to walk away as a budding accountant. You don't need to be an accountant to understand and use the financial information about your business. You need to know enough to keep track of how you're going, extract the information you need when you need it and, most importantly, use that financial information to make the best decisions you can.

Your financial reports are a view of the past. They tell you if all the things you did (or didn't do) produced the financial results you wanted. That said, they have future application: by tracking the past, you can make decisions to produce a better result in the future.

To help you understand the financials, I will walk you through the basics and gradually increase the complexity. You may well have a strong understanding of your financials already but I always believe the occasional refresher is not a bad thing.

We will go through the financial statements demonstrating how they develop and can become more detailed and complex as your business grows and changes.

Non-negotiable financial 'rules'

Let's start with a few key concepts that any small business should consider.

1. Don't do it all yourself

Get an experienced bookkeeper or accountant to prepare your financial reports and advise you on taxation. As mentioned, this is to help you but not let you off the hook. A bookkeeper will cost you money. An accountant will cost you more. Getting your financials wrong, including taxation, could destroy your business. Even if you're one of those owners who loves doing it, and is good at it, it's always preferable to have a second set of eyes.

2. Separate business and personal money

No matter which business structure you choose, you need to very clearly define the lines between you and the business. If you blur these lines, you can find yourself in a mess as time goes on. Small business, especially sole traders, frequently have very blurred lines between business finances and personal finances. You need to be disciplined in separating the two. Record all movements of money between you and the business. This separation also goes to the heart of separating the business risks from your personal risks.

3. Keep good records

When you spend money on the business, keep your receipts. Record what the purchases were and where you spent that money. Use the business debit or credit card for business purchases. Track all cash purchases. The amounts may be small, but the discipline is critical and every dollar counts. You should have access to up-to-date accounts, preferably every month. If you are relying on the accountant providing these to you at the end of the year, you could be operating in the dark, financially, for most of the year.

4. Put systems and processes in place that work for you

Consider the accounting system you might want to use. While you may actively involve your accountant in your business, there are some excellent and relatively low-cost accounting software packages on the market that allow you to do a lot more yourself.

5. Pay the taxman

Tax is a very dry and unattractive topic for any business, but the price of getting it wrong can be huge. Sadly, there are too many small businesses that are no longer in business purely because they let their taxes get out of control.

6. Chase every dollar owed to you — vigorously!

I don't think I need to tell you how hard you must work to make money in your business. When you provide your customers with a product or service, you deserve to be paid and should treasure every one of your hard-earned dollars.

You may get paid for your products or services on the spot, like a retail shop or hot-dog stand. You may send your customer an invoice and expect to get paid some time later.

Basically, you are offering them interest-free credit.

Too often, your customers may not pay on time, for any number of reasons. They could be sloppy or disorganised. They could be deliberately using you as their 'bank', keeping your money as long as possible for their own use. They could have their own financial problems. They may have no intention of paying you. Worst of all, they could be in serious financial trouble and you may never see your money.

Let's discuss a few very important considerations, to give you the best chance of getting every dollar owed to you.

- ■ *Include your payment terms with every transaction*
  The payment terms you attach to each of your invoices (sometimes called Terms of Trade) set out your expectations. If you have a hot-dog stand or a retail shop, or if you are paid in cash or on the spot, you normally don't need them. If you do offer credit, you should avoid commencing the service without first providing your customer with your payment terms. Typically your payment terms would include:
  - Within how many days you require payment after the customer receives your invoice (typically 7, 14 or 30 days)
  - What penalty charges you will impose on them if they are late
  - What permissions you require from the customer to check the credit-worthiness before commencing work (privacy issues may exist)
  - Who you might use if they refuse to pay (for example, a debt collector).

  You may feel really uncomfortable asking a trusted customer to sign such a document. In most cases you won't need to enforce it. However, I believe most people in business are very aware of the issues around being paid and would not be surprised by your request. Many customers will like the certainty it brings. If a customer is not prepared to sign, you need to ask why. Perhaps they are someone you can't risk working for. Enlist an experienced person (such as a lawyer) to draw up your payment terms. You should only need to do this once, as you can use them for every transaction after that.

- ■ *Chase the people who owe you money*
  Put in place a process that allows you to record exactly when money is due. Many of the latest accounting and bookkeeping packages provide this. If people are late, politely remind them, as it may simply be an oversight. The longer they delay paying you, the more robust you may need to be in chasing your money. How robust will depend on your relationship with that customer and the circumstances of the late payment. They may be a long-standing or valuable customer who you are confident will pay eventually. Whatever the circumstances, stay on top of this. If you have good payment terms and the situation deteriorates, you will be in a much better position to take more formal action to get your money. You may really hate this process. Don't worry, most people do. Just remember, it is *your* money and your business needs it to survive and thrive.

■ *A few other ideas*

These are a few additional tips that you may consider to assist in ensuring you get paid:

- Find ways that may be accepted by your customers to pay in part or in full up-front.
- Offer discounts for early payments.
- Don't be afraid to check a company's credit-worthiness, especially if the job involves more money than normal or they are strangers to you. Sometimes a rumour about the type of payer they are may also trigger this.
- Check if your bank has more automated and mobile ways to pay. Many banks are implementing ways to help people get paid on the spot using their mobile device and the customer's credit card. Ask your bank.

7. Pay your bills on time

You want your customers to pay you on time, so you too should pay your suppliers on time. You really don't want to get a reputation for being a bad or late payer. At best, it will impact your reputation. Worse, it could result in suppliers reporting you to credit agencies, resulting in a downgrade of your credit rating. They could refuse to supply you any more, which could shut you down. They could also take legal action or push to get you liquidated, so they can get their money, even if you are solvent.

If you have a strong relationship with your suppliers, and pay them on time, they are more likely to lend you a little slack if you do genuinely face a shortage of cash.

Similarly, if you are struggling to meet bank payments, talk to your bank manager. While they want their money repaid, they gain little by letting you fail. If you are struggling to meet your commitments and not talking to them, they will see this as undesirable behaviour and start monitoring you more closely. The fear is they may step in if you have not been talking to them.

8. Cash really is king

I have been asked many times by customers what is the one thing they should do to manage their finances. While I say there are many more than just one, if you had to choose, look at the cash sitting in your bank account every day and know what's going to come out and what is supposed to be coming in. If the money in the bank is disappearing faster than you can top it up, it's pretty obvious where things will ultimately end for you.

Managing your taxes

You will see references to taxation in the profit and loss statement. Understanding and managing the taxes you owe is really important so we need to discuss principles around taxation. In New Zealand about 10 businesses go into liquidation every day. The most common reason this happens is unpaid taxes. This is not because the tax process is unfair, overly difficult, unclear, or that the tax department is going out of its way to close businesses. It is because small businesses are not putting processes in place to manage their taxation. This is not a trend that is unique to New Zealand. It is common throughout the world.

You do need to understand your obligations.

The most common types of taxation to consider in running a small business is Goods and Services Tax (GST) (or the equivalent consumption tax in the country you reside), taxation on the profits you make, typically called provisional tax, and the taxation you have to pay on behalf of your staff (Pay As You Earn, PAYE).

Your taxes may have to be paid in instalments some months after they were incurred. You could have to pay your current year taxes based on previous years earnings, again in amounts spread across the year. As a result, you may have to keep money aside to meet a tax return at some later date. Don't fall into the trap of forgetting this. The taxman will inform you that you owe money, so make sure you haven't spent it on something else.

The tax department (Inland Revenue or IRD) will be vigilant in pursuing businesses that don't pay their taxes. This is the area you should seek help on from the experts if you are unclear of your obligations. Find out what you have to pay, when you have to pay it, and then make absolutely sure it's happening. If you have difficulty paying, talk to the IRD as soon as you can. They may discuss payment options that are manageable.

While you should not let tax decisions drive your business decisions, it would be wise to do all you legally can to reduce the tax you pay.

Many small businesses starting out may not make much money in the initial years of running so are not faced with paying much, if any, tax. As they grow, sales increase and profits follow (which is great), they don't put the processes in place to manage the taxation they will now face. Instead of putting the cash aside to pay tax they use it to buy more equipment, fund growth, pay staff, or cover other planned or unexpected costs.

Often taxation does not have to be paid immediately but some months after it has been incurred. Owners prioritise all other spending putting off the tax that is due, or losing sight of it, only to be faced with a large, and sometimes unexpected tax bill. Once small business get into this cycle it is very difficult to get out of. The IRD is likely to impose interest and penalties on unpaid taxes. If cash is already tight it only adds greater pressure.

If you are faced with being unable to pay your taxes when they are due DON'T ignore this or put the problem off hoping everything will turn out OK. Speak to the IRD as soon as you can and find out your options. If you ask for help they are likely to support you. If you ignore them, and hope the problem goes away, you might face a very disgruntled IRD with no patience. So what can you do to avoid this situation?

- Speak to your tax advisor or accountant to ensure you fully understand the taxes you must pay. You don't need to be an expert but you need to use the experts.
- Remember a percentage of your sales is GST and it is not your money – it belongs to the IRD. In New Zealand 15% or all your sales are GST and you need to put that aside every month, preferably in a separate bank account assigned to pay taxes.

- The tax on your profits (provisional tax) is often paid well after the profits are made. Therefore, find out what they are likely to be from your tax advisor and when they are due.
- Put an extra few percent aside for provisional tax.
- Keep track of your tax obligations every month.
- If you strike problems meeting your tax obligations ask your tax advisor for options and talk to the IRD.

Goods and Services Tax (GST)

GST is what is called a consumption tax. It is including on what you sell and the things you buy. Similar tax exists in other countries and might be called sales tax or value-aded tax.

Understanding and managing GST is very important. It can get a lot of small businesses into serious trouble if it is not managed well. If you are registered to pay GST (in New Zealand you have to be if you are earning more than $60,000 in sales) all your sales will include 15% GST. This is not your money and you need to set it aside as you will need to pay the IRD. Likewise, the products and services you buty will have GST included. You are entited to claim this back. If you sell more than you buy you will be paying the IRD GST when it is due. If you buy more than you make you will get a refund (but remember if this situation exists you are making a loss in the business)

A journey through your financial statements

Let's go back to Michelle, using the birth and steady growth of her solo business to help explain financial statements. While Michelle's business is fictional, she is representative of many businesses (and owners) with whom I've worked. Her situation is common so it should give you a good feel for how the small business financials will look.

Profit and loss statement

Let's look at the first financial statement known as the **Profit and Loss Statement**. The profit and loss statement shows you what money you have made and spent over a defined period, typically a year. Ideally you should review your profit and loss every month.

Cash versus accrual accounting

There are two ways your financial statements could be developed — using cash accounting or accrual accounting. You don't need to decide which to use. You should instead discuss this with your accountant. However, you need to understand which method has been used for your accounts as it can make a difference to how you interpret them and how you respond to them.

- In **Cash Accounting**, you only record transactions in your profit and loss statement when the money comes into or out of the business as cash.

- In *Accrual Accounting*, you record transactions as they occur, even though you have not received cash in the case of a sale or paid the cash in the case of a purchase.

In the long run, the two methods will line up. However, they differ on when the money is recorded as coming in and going out of the business.

Why use accrual accounting?

The method that would seem simplest and most obvious is cash accounting, yet it's the least common method used in business. In the end, aren't you only interested when the cash arrives or leaves the business? While that's correct, if you pay on credit and offer credit to customers, your sales and purchases will not line up each month and will make your financial accounts confusing.

When you use accrual accounting, your profit and loss statement records all your sales and all your expenditures at the time you make the sale or receive the goods or services, even if money is yet to pass hands. This is of particular use in the case when you buy and sell using credit. Cash accounting cannot account correctly for inventory. The two methods may produce different tax results so your accountant will need to advise you on the choice for tax purposes. So now let's take a look at Michelle's financial situation.

Michelle's Organic Soaps
Year 1

When Michelle set up her business she set aside $5,000 of her own cash for the business. She still works from home. She needs to do a lot of driving for the business so she has transferred her $5,000 car into the business.

She starts selling her products in the local markets once a month. She has to pay $300 to secure the site at the fair for 12 months. She also sells her products through a small local store.

She sells her products for $10 each. She knows that all the materials that go into making her products cost $7 per product.

She only buys the materials as she needs them. In her first year, her sales exceed her expectations. She sells 1,000 of her products.

So what has Michelle made in her first year?

Sales (1,000 at $10 each)	$10,000
Cost of those Sales (1,000 at $7 each)	$7,000
Gross Profit (or Gross Margin)	$3,000

Definitions

Here are some definitions of what you'll see in your profit and loss statement.

REVENUE   The total of all money made from sales in your business before any costs are taken out. Sometimes you may hear it described as your business *Turnover*. In Michelle's case, her revenue in year one is $10,000.

COST OF SALES (COS)   The costs that you can directly attribute to the revenue or sales you have earned. The costs to produce your products. These are sometimes called the *Cost of Goods Sold*. For Michelle, this is $7,000.

If your business does not sell products but provides a service, this is often called *Cost of Services*. If your service relies entirely on your time, you may have no cost of services. When you don't have work and are not putting any hours in to deliver to customers, you don't have any revenue.

If you stopped producing those products, you would not have the revenue or these costs. Therefore, these are *Variable Costs*.

GROSS PROFIT   If you subtract revenue from the cost of sales, you are left with the gross profit. (This is also called *Gross Margin*.)

In Michelle's case, she has a gross profit of $3,000.

Michelle's Organic Soaps
Expenses
Year 1

Michelle has a number of costs to pay irrespective of the number of products she sells. These are called *Overhead Expenses*, *Overheads* or simply *Expenses*. They include the motor vehicle, accountant and rent on the stall. If you take account of these, you reach her earnings. Michelle's profit and loss statement in her first year is quite simple:

Sales	$10,000
Cost of Sales	$7,000
Gross Profit	$3,000
Expenses	
Motor Vehicle	$400
Accountant	$600
Rent for Market Stall	$300
Total Expenses	$1,300
Earnings (EBITDA)	$1,700

After all this, Michelle has $1,700 of earnings, although this excludes three other key items: depreciation, interest (if any), and taxes.

Definitions

EXPENSES   The costs that have to be paid no matter what the business is producing. These are called **Fixed Costs**. Michelle's fixed costs, at this stage in her business, are very simple. As your business becomes more complex or grows, it will attract a lot more fixed costs. Typical fixed costs in a small business could include:

- Computer maintenance
- Domain hosting
- Software licences and subscriptions
- Travel
- Entertainment (e.g. coffee with customers)
- Training courses
- Printing and stationery
- Wages for permanent administrative staff
- Rent on your office
- Advertising
- Credit card fees
- Insurances
- Legal expenses
- Telephone.

EBITDA   This is an abbreviation for Earnings Before Interest, Taxation Depreciation and Amortisation.

Hopefully, you have found this reasonably simple to this point. While we have still a lot more to cover, it is very important that you are comfortable with these concepts first. **Revenue**, **COS**, and **Expenses** go to the heart of your small business's financial success. They are the three items you have most ability to influence. Let's finish by defining the remaining key items in Michelle's profit and loss statement (see opposite page).

Definitions

INTEREST   Any money the business may be paying on loans or any borrowings.

TAXATION   You will need to check if the financial statements you are reading include or exclude GST. Reports can be prepared either way and you need to ensure you know which format they are in. The money the business has to pay to the government tax office on its earnings. The tax rates, the tax rules, and how and when you pay your taxes will be different from country to country. They may also vary depending on the type of business.

DEPRECIATION   Many of the assets you have purchased in your business will age. When they age they will also reduce in value. If you decided to sell an asset

Michelle's Organic Soaps
Total Profit
Year 1

Let's now incorporate interest, tax and depreciation into Michelle's first profit and loss statement.

Revenue	$10,000
Cost of Sales	$7,000
Gross Profit	$3,000
Expenses	
Motor Vehicle	$400
Accountant	$600
Rent for Market Stall	$300
Total Expenses	$1,300
Earnings	$1,700
Interest (She has no loans as yet)	$0
Depreciation (On her car)	$1,000
Total Profit Before Tax	$700
Taxation	$210*
Net Profit (After Tax)	$490

* I used a tax rate of 30% in this example. It may bear no resemblance to what you may face.

some years after its purchase, it is very likely you will receive far less for it than what you paid for it. It would seem only fair for this to be taken into account in your financial statements. This is **Depreciation**.

Your tax agency will have defined rules guiding how fast you are allowed to depreciate your assets (e.g. a computer vs a motor vehicle). They will also have different rules on the method you use to calculate the depreciation. For example, should you depreciate the asset faster at the start of its life or the same each year?

After you have calculated the depreciation, the value of the asset will be reduced (in your balance sheet). The amount the asset depreciates is considered an expense and is included in your profit and loss statement. It will reduce your profit and consequently your tax.

The key point to remember with depreciation is that no money passes hands. It is purely an accounting calculation, but it does effect your profit and, therefore, your tax, and it will also reduce the value of your assets. It is also worth noting that the value of each asset as it is depreciated each year may not reflect what it is actually worth if you wanted to sell it. The value of the asset in your financial statements is its *Book Value*. What someone is prepared to pay for it may be very different. This is the *Market Value*.

AMORTISATION Similar concept to depreciation but applied to intangible assets such as intellectual property like trademarks and patents.

NET PROFIT AFTER TAX (NPAT) Well, you've reached it — *The Bottom Line*. The word 'net' is included as it indicates the profit is net (after everything has been considered).

Balance Sheet

The **balance sheet** provides details of what the business owns and what it owes to others at a specific point in time. The profit and loss looks at the income and costs over an entire period like a tax or financial year or monthly. The balance sheet is a snapshot in time.

If you compared the growth of your small business to a fruit tree, the root system and the tree trunk would be the balance sheet. The fruit it does (or doesn't) produce each year would be the profit (or loss). A healthy balance balance sheet, like a healthy trunk and root system on a tree, is more likely to help to help you get through the years the business is not producing as much fruit. Let's go through a few key concepts of the balance sheet, such as assets, liabilities and equity.

- **Assets — what the business OWNS.**
- **Liabilities — what the business OWES.**
- **Equity — what remains that belongs to the owners of the business.**

The balance sheet is so called because the following formula must balance every time:

ASSETS = LIABILITIES + EQUITY

Definitions

Let's define these a little better in simple terms:

ASSETS The items within the business that the business owns. They can be

Tangible Assets like cash in the bank, motor vehicles, property, plant, office equipment, and so on. They can also be *Intangible Assets* like patents, copyrights, trademarks and other intellectual properties. Each tax authority will define what you can call an asset and what can simply be included as an expense on your profit and loss statement.

In New Zealand an asset is defined as anything that the business owns that is greater than $500 in value and will last more than a year. Anything less than that is considered an expense that you include in the profit and loss statement.

LIABILITIES

Everything you owe to anybody else at the time the balance sheet is prepared. They include outstanding credit card amounts, loans to a bank, loans to you or family members (if you lent the business money) and money you owe your suppliers.

EQUITY

After what your business owes (liabilities) is taken out from what the business owns (assets), what is left is the owner's equity. Otherwise put, equity is what the business owner owns.

The best analogy is your home. Say you have a home worth $500,000. You still owe the bank $300,000 but you have paid off $200,000. Therefore, the asset is $500,000, liabilities $300,000 and equity $200,000.

Another way to look at equity is the amount left if you sold all the assets for the book values listed in the balance sheet and paid off all your debts.

Equity will come from the earnings retained in the business from its activities in previous years or from funds introduced by the owners.

These can be left in the business or accessed by the owners as *Dividends* (or *Drawings*) from the business. While the owners can draw money from the business, it should be done carefully. If the owners take more out than is in the business, it will remove funds that are important to sustain the business. It makes lenders very nervous as there is no guarantee the owners will put that money back into the business. Only take out what the business can afford.

If you or another partner to the business decide to put more equity into the business (as opposed to the business borrowing money), this account will go up. These will be called *Funds Introduced*.

This is also often called **Stockholders' Equity**, **Shareholders' Equity**, **Owners' Equity**, or **Net Worth**.

Below is Michelle's balance sheet for year one.

A few points to note, before we go further.

- You will notice that the new asset value of the car is $4,000. That is $5,000 less depreciation of $1,000. So after 12 months of use, we have estimated how much it has deteriorated and included a new book value. If Michelle wanted to sell the car, what she could get could be very different.
- The cash put in the bank from the proceeds of Michelle's first year are not the same as Net Profit After Tax ($1,500 versus $500). NPAT includes the depreciation. This is not cash so it can't be included in the cash that is put in the bank.
- Even though the car has depreciated in value to the business, the business has not paid off any of this money (to Michelle) from when the business first took ownership of the car. So the business still owes the full amount, namely $5,000.
- Michelle lent the company $5,000 cash, which is now an asset to the business. However, the business has not paid Michelle back for this so the business has another $5,000 liability.

Michelle's Organic Soaps
Balance Sheet
Year 1
What her business owns and what it owes

ASSETS

Cash — Initial Invested	$5,000
Cash — From Operations	$1,500
Motor Vehicle	$4,000
Total Assets	**$10,500**

LIABILITIES

Money Owed to Owner — Car	$5,000
Money Owed to Owner — Cash	$5,000
Total Liabilities	**$10,000**

EQUITY

Retained Earnings	**$500**

Therefore, it balances.

- If Michelle's business sold off all its assets and paid off all its liabilities (at book value), it would be left with $500. So this is the equity in the business.

Michelle's Financial Results for Year 2

Before we complete Michelle's financials for the second year, stop and ask yourself how you think she has gone at the end of her second year, having done all the above at the start of year two. She has increased sales by a huge amount in the 12 months. She has taken on staff, although she may need more help in light of the hours she is working. She has had to take on some debt to access more cash. She has had to increase her expenses to deliver this growth, including advertising.

Is this a feeling you have? You are so busy chasing work and delivering to your customers that it's hard to pin down what money is coming in and what money is going out. You do, however, still believe you're making sound decisions through the year.

This is the case for Michelle. On the surface, all her decisions seem sound considering the growth in her turnover and potential for even more growth.

But what does the bottom line look like with all these new, more complex moving parts? Let's complete the profit and loss and balance sheets for year two.

Definitions

Firstly, let's make sure you understand the new terms I've introduced:

CURRENT ASSETS	Assets that are expected to convert into cash within one year in the normal course of business. They include cash, accounts receivable and inventory.
NON-CURRENT ASSETS	The business's long-term assets that will last beyond one year. Typically include plant and equipment, motor vehicles, property and intellectual property.
CURRENT LIABILITIES	The business's debts and other obligations that are due to be paid within one year. They include any short-term debt, overdrafts and accounts payable.
NON-CURRENT LIABILITIES	The business's debts and other obligations that are due to be paid beyond one year. They can include long-term loans from the bank or from owners.
OVERDRAFT	A lending facility a bank offers that allows you to take more money out of your account than you put in, meaning it can become overdrawn. There will be limits on how overdrawn it can become and they usually attract higher interest rates.

Michelle's Organic Soaps
Profit and Loss
Year 2

Sales (9,000)	$90,000
Materials Purchased (10,000)	$70,000
Closing Stock (1,000)	$7,000
Cost of Sales	$63,000
Gross Profit	$27,000

Expenses

Wages	$15,000
Lawyers (for TM)	$500
Accountant	$600
Motor Vehicle Running Costs	$400
Web Hosting	$100
Computer Maintenance	$150
Advertising	$500
Rent	$5,000
Total Expenses	**$22,250**

EBITDA	**$4,750**

Interest

Overdraft (10% on $15,000)	$1,500
Depreciation	$2,140
Total Profit Before Tax	*$1,110*
Taxation	$250**

Net Profit (after Tax)	**$860**

Depreciation Calculation (all depreciated over 5 years)			
	Start Value	**Depreciation**	**End Value**
Motor Vehicle	$4,000	$1,000	$3,000
Website	$2,000	$400	$1,600
Computer	$2,000	$400	$1,600
Furniture	$700	$140	$560
Plant and Equipment	$1,000	$200	$800
TOTAL		**$2,140**	

** I conveniently changed the nominal tax rate from 30% to 22.5% in year 2 just to keep the math a little simpler. I doubt you will see such a generous reduction.

Michelle's Organic Soaps
Balance Sheet
Year 2

ASSETS

Current Assets

Cash	$5,400
Accounts Receivable	$15,000
Inventory (Closing 1,000 @ $7)	$7,000
Total Current Assets	**$27,400**

Non-Current Assets

Motor Vehicles	$3,000
Website	$1,600
Computer	$1,600
Furniture	$560
Plant and Equipment	$800
Intangibles — Trademark	$400
Total Non-Current Assets	**$7,960**
Total Assets	**$35,360**

LIABILITIES

Current Liabilities

Accounts Payable	$10,000
Overdraft	$15,000
Total Current Liabilities	**$25,000**

Non-Current Liabilities

Loans from Owner — Car	$5,000
Loans from Owner — Cash	$5,000
Total Non-Current Liabilities	**$10,000**
Total Liabilities	**$35,000**

EQUITY

Retained Earnings (Prior Year)	$500
Retained Earnings (This Year)	$860
Payment to Owner	-$1,000
Total Equity	**$360**

Therefore, it balances.

Assets ($35,360) = Liabilities ($35,000) + Equity ($360)

They are especially helpful for a business that has monthly swings in working capital.

WORKING CAPITAL	The cash the business has access to for its day-to-day operations. It is calculated as ***Current Assets – Current Liabilities = Working Capital***. The more cash you have access to, the better will be your working capital.
INVENTORY	Includes materials you purchase and store for later use. You may also produce extra goods that have not been sold.
ACCOUNTS RECEIVABLE	If you offer your goods and services with credit, you produce the goods and pass them to the customer but you don't receive payment for some time later. As this is money owed to the business, it is an asset.

☞ *If you fear you will never receive some of this money it will become a **Bad Debt**. If this is the case, it will reduce your accounts receivable — your assets — and be treated as an expense (i.e. money that has gone out but will never come back again).*

ACCOUNTS PAYABLE	If you buy goods and services with credit, there will be times where you have purchased the goods and received them from your supplier but you have not yet paid for them. As this is money owed by the business to someone else, it is a liability.

Analysing your financials, a little more deeply

Now that you have a better understanding of how to read your financial statements, it is helpful to gauge how you might be going relative to other similar businesses and previous years.

Why look at the information on your balance sheet?

It's more common for small business owners to keep their eye on the profit and loss statement. It reflects the amount of business coming through the door and the costs in the business. Owners tend to leave the balance sheet until the end of the year or leave this for their accountant or bank to worry about.

This is a mistake you should avoid

How is Michelle feeling, and what can she do?

Michelle is feeling a little disillusioned about the numbers she sees at the end of her second year. The profit and loss and balance sheet have not generated the results she expected. She's paid herself a modest dividend ($1000). Her profit is not much better than the first year ($860), even with the larger revenue ($90,000). Michelle's business also owes others a lot more money than in her first year including unpaid taxes which is incurring interest penalties.

This is when the thoughts of self-doubt start surfacing, and questions like, "What's the point?"

Rather than allowing this to become a hook that traps Michelle in a cycle of unproductive thinking, she needs to stay committed to her goals, revisit why she is doing this and then plan for the next steps. The basics of her business are sound but she is experiencing growing pains. She can't ignore these results but she needs to keep some perspective and then start planning her next steps.

There are several reasons you should keep as close an eye on the information that you normally find on your balance sheet as the information on your profit and loss statements. These include:

- The balance sheet shows the underlying strength of your business and this is what will carry you through the years. The hope is you are building up the assets in your business, especially cash. It is hopeful you are reducing the money you owe other people. This then results in you increasing the money you, the owner, has in the business which is your equity. The balance sheet is a snapshot in time. It will be changing daily as cash moves in and out of your business. The longer you wait between your reviews of your balance sheet, the bigger the changes that will have occurred.

- It is common that your profit and loss statement will use accrual accounting. This reflects the sales and the purchases you have made, but not the status of your cash situation. Your balance sheet will provide a clearer picture of your cash situation.

- Too many owners focus too much on their revenue (or turnover), feeling they are doing well based solely on sales, when the true picture could be very different. There is an apt saying: 'Revenue is vanity but cash is king'. Treat with scepticism those who tell you how successful they are based on the size of their turnover. Harder still is to avoid doing the same thing yourself, and using revenue as the benchmark for financial success. It's great for the ego, but means little if your final cash situation, as represented in the balance sheet, is poor.

- The balance sheet will show you the state of your debtors (who owes you money) and your creditors (who you owe money to). You should never lose sight of this.

- The balance sheet is the only place you can go to see how much cash you can get your hands on in a hurry. This is what is called **Liquidity**. Cash is the most 'liquid' asset. A house or your property is not as liquid.
- You could be making a profit and good revenue, but be slipping in and out of **Insolvency** without even knowing it. You are insolvent when there are insufficient assets to cover your liabilities or you are unable to pay your debts when they fall due. The value of your current assets could be falling in value, with reductions in cash. Your liabilities could be increasing, because people aren't paying you on time. The size of your current liabilities could exceed your assets and you might not even know it.
- Any lender (especially the banks) will gauge the health of your business and their appetite to lend you money, not only on profitability, but also on the health of your balance sheet.

Therefore, keep a close eye on your profit and loss statement *and* your balance sheet. The more you look, the more you will become comfortable, and the less time it will take each time you look at it.

Financial ratios

Financial ratios are used by businesses of all sizes to:

- Provide warning signs of issues that may be starting to occur.
- Compare the business with others in the same industry.
- Allow trending of performance over time.

There are many ratios that bigger businesses use. I will cover a selection of the ones I feel are most relevant to your small business.

Liquidity ratios

The following ratios give you a sense of how much liquidity you have and also your solvency.

Current ratio

The current ratio assesses how much cash you can get your hands on if you need it quickly.

If you have built up cash in your bank account from your activities, you can get access to it immediately. If your business owns buildings, land, plant and equipment, it is much more difficult to turn this into cash.

$$\text{Current Ratio (\%)} = \frac{\text{Current Assets}}{\text{Current Liabilities}}$$

You want this ratio to be well above 1.0. You should be concerned if you see this trending downward on a consistent basis.

Michelle's current ratio:

Year 1:   **No current liabilities**
Year 2:   **1.10 ($27,400/25,000)**

This is something she needs to monitor carefully. Getting her customers to pay will be a big help. Reducing her reliance on the overdraft will also help.

Profitability ratios

% Gross Profit — The golden ratio

Of all the ratios that I devote time to with businesses, especially those that require labour and materials to complete each job, or involve applying a mark-up on the price of products, it is the % Gross Profit. When you sell a product or a service, make sure you are making money on each sale. The % Gross Profit gives you an idea of what you will make on your purchases and what you will make for the year. It does not consider your overheads or fixed costs, just your revenue from sales and the costs you incurred to make those sales.

$$\% \text{ Gross Profit} = \frac{(\text{Revenue} - \text{Cost of Sales}) \times 100}{\text{Revenue}}$$

You want this margin to be as high as possible. *Typically, values are between 30 and 50%.* Remember, we haven't yet looked at covering the fixed costs in your business.

If you see growth in revenue but a decline in your % Gross Profit, you need to consider whether the growth is worth pursuing. It may be growth with a disproportionate increase in your costs or you might be discounting your prices to achieve these higher sales.

The temptation when small businesses grow is to offer discounts or special offers to get more sales. This will start reducing the % Gross Profit. In some cases, if the sales volumes are really high because of the discounts offered, this may be OK as the increased sales compensates for the reduced margins. BUT proceed with great caution if you see this margin decreasing over time.

Take a look at the Breakeven discussion a little further on to see how big a difference a reduction in Michelle's % Gross Profit could have on her business. Consider what impact it will have on your business.

This is also a useful exercise to do on each product rather than the whole business. Some products will cost less to make and sell for a higher price. Others may not. You need to be sure the products with a higher margin are not paying for the products with poor or no margin.

% Profit Margin

The profit margin relates to the net profit after tax as a percentage of your revenue. If you have a healthy % Gross Profit but a poor % profit margin, it reflects high fixed costs (expenses).

Sometimes you may hear of a company making huge profits but this does not tell you the full picture. The profit margin adds a little more clarity on this.

$$\% \text{ Profit Margin} = \frac{(\text{Net Profit after Tax}) \times 100}{\text{Revenue}}$$

The hope is that something reasonable is left after everyone has taken his or her piece of your business. You may feel you have had a great year, producing your best revenue ever. You may have done this and still maintained the same % gross margin on every sale you have made. However, it may have required you to take on a lot more fixed costs. You may have had to borrow more, hire staff or you may have had to buy more assets that have must be depreciated.

Michelle's % profit margin:

Year 1:   **4.90%** ($490/$10,000 x 100)
Year 2:   **0.96%** ($860/$90,000 x 100)

Michelle's gross profit is not high enough to cover the high fixed costs she has added to the business. Her profit is nearly zero. We will discuss how little changes in revenue and costs will have a big benefit on Michelle's profit. (See the discussion on 1 + 1 + 1 ≠ 3.)

Breakeven Revenue

If your sales start to fall there will be a point where you will only be covering your expenses (fixed costs) and making no profit However, as your sales fall, so too will your cost of sales. What will remain constant is the % Gross Profit. What is the revenue your small business needs to make to just cover costs?

$$\text{Breakeven Revenue} = \frac{\text{Expenses}}{\% \text{ Gross Margin}}$$

Michelle's breakeven revenue:

Year 1: **$4,333** ($1,300/0.3)
Year 2: **$74,167** ($22,250/0.3)

Michelle needs to sell a great deal more now just to cover her high fixed costs.

👉 *This standard breakeven calculation is only part of the story. It does not include money you need to pay off on any loans, dividends, drawings or funds for new or replacement assets. These come from your balance sheet. You could recalculate your breakeven revenue adding these cash amounts into the expenses, if you intend funding them from your operations. This will result in you needing to make even more to break even.*

If we included the loans a small business owner must pay off, any drawings the owner needs to take from profits, and any assets the owner wishes to buy using the company's assets, the Breakeven Revenue would look more like the following:

$$\text{Breakeven Revenue} = \frac{\text{Expenses+Loans+Drawings+Assets+Tax}}{\text{\% Gross Margin}}$$

This means the revenue the small business owner must make, just to cover all their costs, is much higher. This is a more realistic situation as many small businesses will need to take drawings, borrow money and buy equipment from the profits they make.

Impact of % Gross Profit on Breakeven Revenue

To show you how important an impact a reduction in Michelle's % Gross Profit has on her business's breakeven, let's look at two different scenarios for the third year for Michelle if she continues to grow — one with the same % Gross Profit and one with a reduced % Gross Profit. (see next page)

Scenario 1 — End of Year 3

Sales	=	$150,000
Cost of Sales	=	$105,000
% Gross Profit	=	30%
		(same as last year)

Expenses
Increases from $22,250 to $32,250
(Mid-year)

Revenue (sales) increased AND
Profit Increased

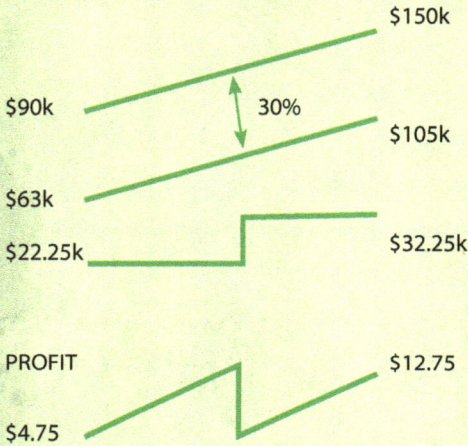

$150k
$90k   30%
$105k
$63k
$22.25k $32.25k

PROFIT $12.75
$4.75

Scenario 2 — End of Year 3

Sales	=	$150,000
Cost of Sales	=	$120,000
% Gross Profit	=	20%
		(worse than last year)

Expenses
Increases from $22,250 to $32,250
(Mid-year)

Revenue (sales) increased BUT
Profit Decreased (Loss)

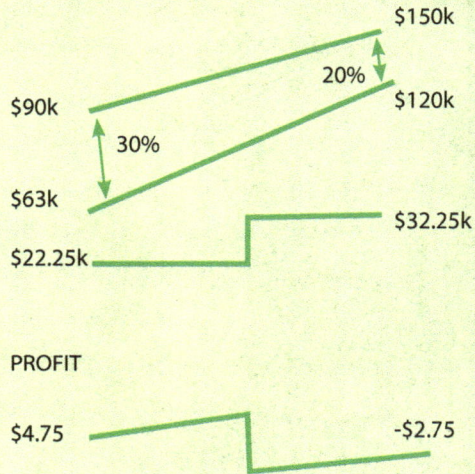

$150k
20%
$90k $120k
30%
$63k
$32.25k
$22.25k

PROFIT
$4.75   -$2.75

Now let's see what Michelle would have to make in sales in Year 3 with the two different scenarios.

Scenario 1 — End of Year 3

Breakeven Revenue = $\frac{\$32,250}{0.3} = \$107,500$

In this scenario Michelle must produce sales of $107,500 to cover her expenses and make a profit.

Scenario 2 — End of Year 3

Breakeven Revenue = $\frac{\$32,250}{0.2} = \$161,250$

In this scenario Michelle must produce sales of $161,250 to cover her expenses and make a profit.

Therefore, with everything else staying the same, Michelle will have to make $53,750 in sales to cover her costs if she lets her %Gross Margin drop from 30% to 20%.

What to do when all you are selling is your time?

You may well run a small business that only offers a service to your customers. This is where people are paying for your skill and expertise rather than buying your products. You may not use any materials in providing that service. In this case, the biggest cost of providing the service is your time. What price do you put on your time?

There are a few things you need to consider and things you must track in running a service based business:

- How much can you charge for each hour you provide? Look back at Pricing in the Four Ps. The same principles apply.
- How many hours can you work in a week? How many hours do you want to work?
- How much time must you set aside to run the business and carry out activities you can't charge the customer for?
- How many hours do you feel you can bill to customers in any week?

Lets now use a simple example of a small business where the only person in the business is the owner and all they offer is their service.

- They work a normal 40 hours per week and have four weeks leave each year. Therefore, the maximum hours they will work in any year is 40 x 48 = 1920 hours/year
- They charge $100/hour for their time, as that is a little below what their competitors charge but the owner feels is a fair hourly rate. This means the most the owner could make in a year is $192,000 (1920 hours x $100/hour)
- The owner spends one day a week (8 hours) doing administration, writing proposals and bookkeeping.
- The owner spends another day each week (8 hours) marketing the business, chasing potential customers and networking.
- Therefore, there are only 24 hours each week the owner charges customers. This generates revenue of $115,200 (24hours/week x 48 weeks x$100/hour)

The difficulty with a service based business is you can only work so many hours, charge so much for those hours to customers and, therefore, the revenue you can make is limited.

In the case of this owner, if they are unhappy with the $115,200 revenue they will need to charge more hours out per week (often called "**Billable Hours**"), work more hours each week, take less holidays, or charge more per hour – or a combination of all of these things.

Some options service based businesses can choose to pursue, other than working more hours, include:

- Look at ways to turn the business's services into products that the owner can sell without requiring their time.
- Employ more people and ensure they bill out more hours to customers.

- Look at ways to offer the service to larger numbers of people (e.g. group training or workshops). You can offer the service at a lower price per person but attract a higher hourly rate.
- Offer packages where you can define greater value than just offering hourly rates – you can then sell the overall value of the outcome of your service not just the hours you put in.

How can you improve the bottom line? ($1 + 1 + 1 \neq 3$)

By completing the above analyses, you will be able to consider more deeply how financially healthy your small business is. Your financial accounts and the ratios I have shown you reflect what has happened in the past. If you are unhappy with the results, you need to understand what has contributed to them so you can change the business to achieve the financial results you seek.

All the above analyses will allow you to ask, and more importantly, answer the following questions:

1. How much am I selling and is it producing sufficient revenue?
2. How well do I understand what it costs to produce each of my products and services?
3. Am I producing good margin on each different product or service and for the business as a whole?
4. Are my fixed costs reasonable or are they eating into my earnings?
5. How can I lift my revenue and reduce my variable and fixed costs without compromising the service to my customers, or core purpose and values?

To show you how even small changes in your revenue and costs can have on your business, carry out the following simple calculation that I call the $1 + 1 + 1 \neq 3$ test:

1. Increase your last annual revenue by 1%.
2. Reduce the related cost of sales by 1%.
3. Reduce your expenses by 1%.
4. Subtract these new costs from the new revenue.

I am very sure the increase in your earnings is much greater than 3% — my guess is it is probably closer to 25%. Imagine the benefits you would see if you could increase revenue by 10 or 20%, especially if you can do it without increasing your cost of sales or expenses.

Budgets and forecasts

As mentioned, your profit and loss and balance sheet look at the past performance of your small business. Based on this, and as part of your business planning, you should develop a budget for the next 12 months. This will guide you on the changes you need to make. It will also help you track whether you are heading in the right direction.

I believe the most critical, and perhaps the only, budget you need to develop is a **Cash Flow Forecast**, as all your actions should be about improving the cash situation.

Whether you use a spreadsheet, features in your accounting software, or a piece of paper are less important than just doing it and keeping it simple.

Write down all the items from your profit and loss statement that involve cash coming in or out of the business. Ignore depreciation, for example.

Below that, list all the cash transactions that will occur on your balance sheet. This could include cash to buy more assets or inventory. It could be to take more dividends (or drawings) from the business. You may wish to introduce extra cash from your own savings or pursue a loan, which will increase your cash.

Michelle's 1 + 1 + 1 ≠ 3 Calculation

Let's use Michelle's second-year results to test this. What if she were able to increase her revenue by 1% (i.e. by $900), reduce her costs by 1% (i.e. $700) and reduce her expenses by 1% (i.e. $223)? What would be the change in her EBITDA and her NPAT?

Her EBITDA increases from $4,750 to $6,572. That is by 38%.

Her NPAT increases from $860 to $2,053. That is by 139%.

If these were 5% or even 10% changes, you can see how significant the improvements could be. Add to this tighter management of her debtors and things could look very different for Michelle in a short space of time. If she fails to act, her huge potential could fade very rapidly.

Once you have written this all down for the next 12 months, break it out into months. Some cash flow items will be the same every month. Some will be one-offs in a certain month of the year.

Remember, it is a forecast and things will change. However, at least it's a start.

Summary

So let's see if we can summarise the accounting aspects of your business.

- Your bottom line is the result of everything else you do in your business.

- Whether you like or dislike keeping an eye on the books doesn't matter. You don't have to be an expert, but you do need to understand and look at them often.
- Follow the simple rules of managing your small businesses' money. Get trusted and good help. Separate out personal spending. Use a good accounting system and keep good records. Pay the taxman. Chase every hard-earned dollar. Pay your bills on time.
- It's a cliché, but seriously, *cash is king*.
- In your profit and loss, know your revenue, cost of sales and expenses.
- Make sure you are making good margin on your sales or you could lose it all in fixed costs.
- Understand and read your balance sheet. All cash flows from your business should end up here.
- If you only offer a service assess what hours you can bill out to customers
- Learn how to analyse the financial statements. Once you have done it a few times, you'll be able to analyse it very quickly in future.

Questions

- How well do you understand the terms revenue, cost of sales, gross profit, depreciation, EBITDA, profit, assets, liabilities and equity?
- Where would you go to find these figures in your financial accounts?
- How do you establish whether your business is financially healthy?
- How are you ensuring you have money set aside to pay all your taxes?
- How would you change your business if it were not as financially healthy as you would like?

Chapter 13
Finding Money from Other Sources

From time to time, you may pursue goals that require you to access external funds.

If your business is generating sufficient cash through sales, this will make more money available for you to do other activities and ventures in the business. If you believe your business has the potential to grow more quickly, it is unlikely that the cash generated from sales will be enough.

You may well have a business that is profitable even if you are not seeking growth. However, you may have large swings in outgoing cash and incoming cash from month to month. In this case, you may need additional funds to provide working capital (i.e. current assets minus current liabilities).

Your business is likely to benefit more from the use of someone else's money to increase the speed of growth than if you used only your own money.

You may be very nervous about seeking external funds as it may bring greater risk. Like anything in business, our actions and decisions have risks. In the case of accessing money from elsewhere, the reward is the activity or growth you can achieve with that additional money. By contrast, though, the risk is it exposes you and your small business if you are unable to repay it.

The key is not to avoid the risk but to assess it; consider the scenarios (good and bad) and make the decision that meets your business's needs at a risk level you can tolerate.

We all have different appetites for risk and this is influenced by our perception of what we stand to lose. You must be able to sleep at night without the burden of worry that may come if you expose yourself to an uncomfortable level of risk. That's why I won't tell you the 'right' level of risk. Only you can gauge that. It's totally individual.

Borrowing money — debt

Using your own savings

As a small business owner, it's likely you have put some of your own savings into your business. You may also have stopped paying yourself much of a salary, compared to the salary you could earn if you worked in someone else's business. This is no different to lending your business money in that you are giving up your normal lifestyle to allow the cash in the business to build up.

Your business should reach a point where you can reclaim that money and also start paying yourself something like a decent salary. You should think of this money as a loan rather than a donation. And you should think of the business as a separate entity to you, even if you are a sole trader.

You are probably going to run out of personal cash to keep injecting into the business. You may simply want to stop putting your own savings into the business and start accessing other funds. At some point, you'll have to look at accessing someone else's money.

Borrowing from friends and family

The next source you can turn to is that rich sibling, parent, uncle or wealthy best friend. This is typically the next most popular source of funds to start up and run a small business, after your own cash.

It is possible this money will come without the same interest charges or restrictions that a bank or other third party may place on you.

Beware. Borrowing from family or friends could create its own unique issues for you. Some family members or friends may believe that lending you money gives them the right to meddle in the affairs of your business. You may have only wanted their money, but ended up with an uninvited partner. This could damage your relationship or your business.

Businesses and close relationships, especially relationships based on love, are not always a good mix. While the family member or friend may have complete trust in you as a person, things may turn rather nasty if you strike problems and can't pay that person back.

You can certainly make this work if you and the family member are completely open about the arrangement at the start and try to keep the business and personal relationships separate. The more you can discuss how you will handle all likely scenarios, the better.

- What if the family member wants or needs the money back early?
- What if you can't meet their repayment requirements?
- Where do they fall in the priorities for being repaid if your business fails?
- What if the family member fears losing their money and wants you to run the business differently?

As I mentioned, all external funds will come with some risks. The risks that come with family of friends lending you money may be a little different to other external funders.

Banks

Banks (or their equivalent) are likely to be your next port of call for money. Borrowing from a bank is probably something you have already done for your house, car and certainly for credit cards. Banks are in the business of lending you money. They will usually do the best they can to achieve this for you. However, they are also in the business of getting their money back. They will expect to be reassured that you will be able to do this, irrespective of the impact getting it back may have on you or your business.

After the events of the global financial crisis, banks around the world have become a little more conservative and risk-averse in their lending. Time will tell if they start relaxing restrictions. Even if they do, remember only to borrow what you need and within the risk appetite you can tolerate. While the global financial crisis could be partly blamed on the behaviour of banks and other financial institutions, it could also be blamed on people borrowing far more than they could afford.

While banks are incentivised to ensure you succeed, very few banks have the capacity to hold your hand and they are unlikely to step in if you need help. Most banks will monitor the behaviour of everyone to whom they lend. They will assess their customers' behaviour in how they meet their loan commitments. If they see a pattern of unacceptable behaviour, they may step in, which is definitely not what you would want to happen.

If you are ever struggling to meet the bank's requirements for the loan(s) you have, talk to them. Often, they will work with you to make repayment more feasible.

All banks have internal boundaries and guidelines to lend money to small businesses. It will depend on the risk appetite of each bank, but typically they will be more comfortable with either some level of security over the business's assets or some form of personal guarantee to give them greater confidence in receiving their money back.

Usually, a personal guarantee will have to be backed by a physical asset. This may be something that you or your business owns, including your home.

We spoke about the protection a Limited Liability Company can give you if your business gets into trouble. Basically, if your business fails, you are likely to be forced to turn all the company's assets into cash (liquidation). If there isn't enough money from this to pay everyone you owe, these people will have to go without. No-one is normally able to touch anything you personally own in this situation. However, the minute you give a personal guarantee over an asset, this protection or security may be at risk.

So why don't you simply say no to the bank's request for that guarantee?

This is what is typically called **unsecured lending**. Some banks simply won't do this and would rather turn you away than take the risk. Others may do it, but they will want to know a great deal about your business before they will even consider it. If they do, it will usually come at a much higher rate of interest and with other requirements, such as reporting regularly on how you are going.

I'm sorry to say that small business owners are not who the banks like lending to without some security. In their eyes, you are statistically more likely to fail, won't borrow as much as the big guys and are likely to be more work for them, relative to the money you borrow. However, if they get security, they are usually more interested. The bank will also want to know you are producing enough cash to service the repayments. Even if you have security, without the cash available you still may not get a loan.

If you are looking to borrow from a bank, shop around. Who offers the best variety of business lending products? Who offers the best deal? Who has the best support for the size of lending you are looking to take on?

The key is not to be so risk-averse as to do nothing. Fully understand your risk, and if you don't understand it, seek the right advice before finalising anything.

Types of bank borrowing for small business

With the deregulation of the banking sector, there are many different types of loans that banks could offer you. I will touch on a few of the most common options that are likely to apply to a business of your size.

Credit cards

I'm sure you know a great deal already about this form of bank borrowing. You may have been able to negotiate a higher limit on your business credit card than you could on your personal credit card.

Your business should have a credit card linked to a bank account that is solely for business purchases and held in your business's name.

It's virtually impossible to not be aware of the very high costs you will face if you fail to meet your monthly repayments. Choose as low a limit as you can manage and make sure you pay the credit card off.

Bank overdraft

I mentioned earlier that your business might need additional working capital. While your credit card can help a little, it might not have a high enough limit for your needs and the interest rates it attracts may be much greater than an overdraft.

If your business has been able to build up good cash reserves, you may decide not to seek any money from the bank for working capital. Yet, banks have been offering business overdraft facilities for many decades. In fact, the first was in the early 1700s. An overdraft is a great way to manage your week-to-week cash needs.

Overdrafts can have high interest rates and you need to be disciplined in paying them back so you don't exceed any limits or they could incur even higher charges. The more you ask for, the more it could cost you, so manage your overdraft to as low a level as you can. Also, you should shop around for the best deal.

Asset financing

Banks, funders or equipment suppliers may lend you money and secure that lending over the specific assets you intend buying with that money. If it is an equipment supplier, they may offer you the financing to allow you to buy their equipment. You pay it back, with interest. If you get into trouble, you may only stand to lose that asset rather than your entire business.

External investment — equity funding

Equity funding is far less common for businesses like yours but still a very important form of funding. It is most often the choice of small business start-ups and businesses with growth potential.

Remember, equity is the part of the business that you and any other shareholders own. By seeking equity funding, essentially you are looking for someone else to take a share in the ownership of your business. A person who takes a share in your business will not receive interest repayments (unlike a bank where they provide you with debt). Also, the investor will not seek personal guarantees. They, like you, are prepared to take on risk, back the business and make their money from its success.

People who want to take some ownership in your business are faced with bigger risks than the bank that lends you money. They will be looking to make a lot more money than they would by simply keeping their money in another investment. Therefore, good investors look for those businesses that have potential to grow and bring a healthy return on the initial investment.

People may also want to invest in your business for reasons other than growth, for instance someone who sees themselves as a successor or someone with a desire to be more deeply involved.

Most investors will want some level of direct involvement in the business, considering the risks they are taking. This could be good or bad, depending on where you may have gaps in your skills, for example. An investor may bring more than just their money, by also bringing experience that you could not otherwise access.

By bringing in an external investor, you can't expect to maintain the same freedom and control as when you're on your own. That's why you need to be extremely careful about who you decide to bring into your business.

There may be some investors who do not want to play an active part in the day-to-day running of the business. They will, however, still want to know what you are doing and are unlikely to let you do anything that may put their investment at risk.

Who else will invest in your business?

Family or friends

After a small business owner uses up their own and their bank's funds, there's a view that they turn to the 'Three Fs' for funding: family, friends and fools. While this may seem a little harsh, it holds merit, but still might be a legitimate option.

We already spoke about turning to family or friends for a loan. There may also be an approach where a family member or friend could buy into your business. The advantage of this is that you know each other before proceeding. They may also be more inclined to invest than would an external investor if significant growth was not your goal.

However, unlike the case of lending, the family or friend now has the right to meddle in the business because they part-own it. It's even more important that you consider the impacts of this arrangement on your relationship before you enter into it. What may start out as an exciting shared adventure could end in a serious break-up of the relationship . . . and the business.

Angel investors

Angel investors are typically business people who have enough personal wealth to invest in high-growth, high-risk businesses. There are likely to be associations or forums nearby that bring angel investors in contact with small businesses seeking funding.

This type of investor is not going to invest in a small business that does not demonstrate significant growth potential. Typically, they will pursue small start-up businesses with international growth potential. They will do their homework not only on the business and its potential, but on you. They may not be investing with the intention of hanging around as long as you may intend or expect. Typically, they are there to get their money back at some point.

Angel investors are definitely not banks. They will want to get involved. As they are usually experienced and financially successful business people, they could bring you a great deal of experience and support as you grow.

They may not put in huge sums (say, $50,000 to $250,000), but they could well be investing in many small businesses to diversify their risk.

Don't expect to walk up to an angel investor and get their money easily. You need to have a very good story, a plan for your business, and a plan for how you intend using their money to generate growth.

The same risks exist in choosing to approach and work with an angel investor as any other type of funding. Don't get dazzled by the money or their credentials. If the person does not fit your business, your values or your goals, remain cautious. Ensure you can work with that person and do your homework on them as much as they do on you.

Other sources of funding

Grants to small businesses

Most developed economies have processes in place to support small business like yours. These come in all shapes and sizes covering a wide range of purposes. They could be anything from government agencies to philanthropic businesses. Look around. Every dollar helps. You may need to complete an application and other paperwork to establish if you are eligible, but it could be worth it. Unfortunately, there are not too many options available in New Zealand, except for businesses with high growth and export potential.

Invoice or debtor financing

This is another source of help with working capital. If your business is paying money to suppliers but your customers don't pay you until many weeks later, invoice financing may be an option to consider. It does not apply to businesses paid in cash or at the point of sale. Unlike the banks, the providers of the invoice financing don't want security over any of your assets. They are relying on getting their money from your customers.

Small companies with rapid growth can also use invoice financing, as they may struggle to keep on top of their payment processes, including making sure they have cash coming through the door when they need it.

This is how it works. The invoice financing company will pay you a large percentage of your outstanding invoices the moment you send them out to your customers. This is typically around 80%. You have cash straight away to continue your business and don't have to stress about waiting for your customers to pay the bill.

When the customer pays the invoice, the invoice finance company gives you the outstanding money, less their fees. These fees vary and can be higher than an overdraft rate.

You may hear it described differently in different places. Debtor financing, invoice financing and receivables financing are all essentially the same thing. Different companies have variations on what they offer. Some manage all your invoices with all your customers and some are prepared to assist with individual invoices. Some will manage your entire payment process, while others leave you to manage all the interactions with your customers and just handle the money part.

You may feel you are too small to use this type of funding, but in reality invoice financing companies may offer this type of financing to businesses of all shapes and sizes.

Like any funding option, you need to ensure you fully understand it. Invoice financing does not increase the amount of cash you have access to; it just ensures you get the cash you are owed straight away.

It can prove more expensive than an overdraft, but should not put personal assets at risk. Many invoice financing companies may offer a more hands-on level of support for your business than would a bank. If you use the invoice financing company to manage all your invoices, it can take a major load off you.

However, it may be costly, as well as putting someone between you and your customers. Also, if you get attached to the invoice financing company, it might make it difficult to take this process back at a later date.

Crowdfunding

Crowdfunding is a relatively new online phenomenon that began in 2005 and has grown alongside online business activity. There are now almost 700 crowdfunding sites around the world, about 200 of which are in the US. The amount of money raised through crowdfunding sites worldwide has grown from $US 530 million in 2009 to $US 2.8 billion in 2012.

A few of the better-known sites include the Snowball Effect and PledgeMe in New Zealand, Kickstarter (USA), IndieGoGo (USA), Seedrs (UK), Crowdcube (UK), and WeFund (UK).

Crowdfunding sites allow you to put your idea up on their website where you request funding from anyone who may be interested in your idea. Typically, you ask for a certain amount of money and people promise small amounts towards that total (as little as $10). If you reach your total, you get the funding, as well as exposure from the process. You can attract more people by gaining their interest in your idea and with promises of something in return. This might be a free sample of your product once it's available.

Some crowdfunding sites are based solely on donations.

Crowdfunding has provided money for films, social causes, music, technologies, literature, and a huge variety of small business ventures. Most people only seek relatively small amounts ($500 to $10,000).

Equity-based crowdfunding

This is another variation on the crowdfunding model. In this case, people are pledging small amounts to buy a share in the business. If you are the small business owner, this could mean you end up with many owners of your business and a whole lot of unnecessary problems. Many countries have been slow to legislate and allow this model. Normally, buying shares in a new business, of any size, is a tightly regulated process. This type of purchase is not regulated; hence some countries' initial unease. It is still in its infancy, but is worth keeping a close eye on, as it grows in acceptance.

Peer-to-peer funding

Peer-to-peer or person-to-person (P2P) funding is another relatively new online source of funding.

In this case, borrowers and lenders interact directly through a website. The borrower requests money and the lender lends directly to the person without the involvement of a bank. It is often a cheaper source of borrowing. Lenders still expect to see evidence of your credit-worthiness.

Examples of P2P lending sites include Prosper.com and the LendingClub.com in the USA and Zopa.com in the United Kingdom. Zopa claims it has lent more than £580 million.

Not all countries allow this form of lending, although it is also slowly gaining wider acceptance and worth following to see how it progresses.

Summary

These are the key points to consider when you are seeking additional funding:

- You are likely to be the first source of funds for your business. Think of it as a loan that you want back later with interest.
- Friends and family may lend you money, but be cautious about this damaging a long-standing relationship.
- Banks have a wide range of lending options for businesses, so shop around and see what lending arrangement best suits you.
- Banks are in the business of lending and getting their money back. Be sure you fully understand the personal guarantees and securities they require before you borrow.
- There are investors who may want to take a share in your company. The more sophisticated investors (like angel investors) will want to see strong growth potential and a very good business story provided by a competent owner.

- There are also legitimate non-bank options to access funds including invoice financing as well as a growing number of online options.
- Remember, before asking for money, know what it is for. What impact (good and bad) will it have on the business? Stay within your risk appetite. If you do this, access to someone else's money could make a huge difference.

Questions

- What level of working capital (ie cash) do you need to run your business?
- What level of external funding do you need to achieve your goals?
- Where would you go for external funding?
- How confident are you that external parties will provide you with funding?

Chapter 14

What's Your Business Worth?

While you may have no intention of selling your small business or buying another business, it is still important to understand how to establish the value of a business, including your own. The factors that increase its market value are also factors that will greatly improve your business.

The processes to value a small business are often misunderstood and I've seen many examples where this has led to heartache. So be warned! To illustrate, here are a few illustrations of what could happen from some real events:

1. A business with three employees sold products to a chain of well-known and popular retail shops. They were keen to sell the business after almost 10 years. They were of the view that the contracts with the retail shops had real value to any buyer. Yet, the retail shops continually squeezed them on price, which impacted the small business's profitability. Their margins were very small leading to limited earnings. They had no negotiating power with retail shops that were in a position to cease buying the owner's products at any time they chose. They pursued an independent valuation but, to their amazement, found the value to be near zero. They would only get small amounts of cash if they sold some of their assets and inventory. They were shattered to hear their business was basically worthless after all the effort they had put in.

2. Two owners invested well over $ 400,000 of their own savings to research and develop a high-tech patented product. They had also built up $US 100,000 in stock to sell the devices and components through their website. Their market research indicated there was potential for significant international growth for their products. However, after five years in business, this had not translated into sales. Profits were modest and also volatile from year to year. They required several staff to manage, pack and ship products, which meant they had high fixed costs. An investor expressed interest based on the market potential. However, the investor valued the business at less than $US 500,000, focusing on historic sales and a projection of future sales. There would also be a need for some effort to improve the business after sale. The owners thought it was worth more than $US 2 million and the investment didn't go ahead.

3. Two partners had been in a consultancy business for almost 20 years. One partner decided he wanted to retire. Under the shareholders agreement, the remaining partner had first right to buy the departing partner's share. He was keen to do this and keep the business going for a few more years, possibly passing it on to his son thereafter. However, there was no process outlined in the shareholders agreement on how to value the business in this situation. There was a significant difference in the two parties' views on value. It was eventually put in the hands of lawyers to solve the dispute around valuation and a 20-year relationship was destroyed.

There are various methods of valuing small businesses, but none is an exact science. They are opinions. Often the greatest skill in valuing a business is research and curiosity rather than analytical skills. The greater your knowledge of the type of business and market you want to buy or sell in, the better.

One of the biggest uncertainties in the valuation process comes because you will be trying to predict the future. What has occurred in the past may guarantee little about the future. I always recommend that you use experts who are active in the sale and purchase of businesses in your region so that you tap into up-to-date expertise. This will also offer you an independent and objective result, free of emotional attachment.

Even though I recommend you use third parties in this process, at the appropriate time, you should still understand the process for valuing a business yourself. This may save you time and costs in getting valuations when you are doing an initial scan of the market. It will also allow you to self-evaluate to see if you are increasing your business's value. In the end, the value that is settled on in a market sale is only decided by what the buyer and seller agree.

Valuation methods

The method I will detail here is the method I have seen most commonly used to buy or sell a business in the open market where it's the intention to keep the business going after the sale (as a going concern). There are variations on this valuation process for businesses that need to be liquidated or where an existing shareholder wants to buy (or sell) part of the business.

Historical earnings method

The historical earnings method looks at how profitable the business has been over the previous few years. While this does not guarantee the business will continue to be as profitable after the purchase, it provides a great insight into the business. In the end, whoever is buying is doing so to achieve a financial return. Therefore, tracking the financial performance and projecting this into the future is the ultimate test. It does not consider the value of the assets in the business. It is only concerned with the profitability provided by those assets.

This method relies heavily on the accuracy of the historical financial reports. You should only use those accounts that were prepared by an accountant or trained bookkeeper and (usually) those that have been used for tax purposes. Proceed cautiously with the valuation if the financials are abbreviated, out of date or in a poor state.

Adjusted average profit (or earnings)

From the accounts, establish the average profit over the previous three (or more) years.

You should look more closely at what makes up the profit, as it may be hiding factors that will impact the new owner's profitability. Establish the likely future earnings. In valuations, these are often called *future maintainable earnings*.

Once you have done all the adjustments, some of which I will cover below, the best earnings figure from the profit and loss statement to use for the valuation is EBITDA. This separates out taxation and interest issues from the genuine business issues.

Some adjustments you need to consider:

1. **Owner's salary and drawings**

   Many owners of small businesses do not take a salary or drawings in a way that reflects any sensible market rate. Owners may also have many family members working in the business for little or no money. If you were to replace all these people with a single salaried owner, being paid something consistent with the market rate, it could have a very different result on the earnings.

2. **Other activities not done at market rates**

   There may be other items in the financials that do not reflect the market rate that a new owner may have to pay. For example, the business may be housed in a building that is owned by the current owner's family. The current owner is paying a heavily discounted level of rent. The building is not part of the sale. Any new owner may be forced to pay full rent.

3. **One-off revenues or costs**

   There may be events in the past financials that were one-offs and are unlikely to occur again. These could be both in revenue and in costs. You should consider removing these or they may distort the valuation.

4. **Inconsistency in the financial results over each year**

   You may find that the financial results have differed greatly over the years. This could be a consistent climb or decline in performance or volatility from year to year. You will need to dig more deeply to understand what this means. If the earnings have grown or reduced over the years, you will need to ascertain if this is likely to continue. If the results are volatile, which year will reflect the most likely future result?

Considerations other than profitability

Transferability

An important factor that needs to be considered in the sale of a small business is how transferable it is. As we have covered throughout this book, a small business is heavily reliant on the owner. In many cases, this reliance is so great it removes any chance of a sale, no matter how strong the profitability has been. Those owners who can make the business more independent of themselves are the ones most able to increase the business's value and generate a sale.

Will the transfer be unencumbered?

If the business has assets that are tied to borrowings, this makes the sale far less attractive. Sales are often on the basis that the business is not encumbered by creditors' claims (including bank debt) or any security over assets. An unencumbered asset is much easier to sell or transfer than one with an encumbrance.

What are the future prospects for the business?

The buyer of a business is likely to be looking for a business that can be purchased at a lower price and then grown in value beyond what the current owner could manage. Basically, purchase the business at a discount then step in and realise its true potential. Buying a business at a discounted price might be possible if the existing business has not been managed well or the owner is forced to sell below market price for personal reasons.

How the buyer and seller see the future potential of the business and how the buyer and seller perceive the business is being managed may differ and impact on each party's view of its value.

If the current owner believes future sales will be much greater than the past financial performance indicates, they may seek a higher price before selling. The buyer will need to consider this when negotiating the final price. Is the future potential real and worth paying a premium, especially if someone new is managing it?

The buyer might say that they are not prepared to pay a premium because the only way the business can truly realise its value in the future is if it is in the hands of new management. That being the case, why should the current owner see that reflected in the sale price?

The future, risk, and The Multiplier

With a one-year future maintainable earnings estimate, you can ask yourself some further important questions in determining the value of the business:

- How far into the future should you consider?
- How many years ahead do you expect these earnings to continue?
- Will earnings grow, decrease or stay about the same?
- How long will this business remain in business?
- How soon would a buyer want to pay back the money invested in the business from future earnings produced by this business?
- In comparing two similar businesses for sale, which one is riskier, and how does that affect the value?
- How do you relate earnings to the final value of the business?

Basically, by how much should a single year of maintainable earnings be multiplied to determine the final estimate of value? This is very much an assessment of the risk.

The number by which you multiply the maintainable earnings is often called ***The Multiplier***. The Multiplier is a rule of thumb and involves judgment. Those who actively value businesses on a regular basis can determine **The Multiplier** with some accuracy.

☞ *The process to determine the total value of the business by projecting current earnings into the future to establish what the business is worth now is also called the **Capitalisation of Future Maintainable Earnings.***

Factors to consider in determining The Multiplier:

- There may be conventions for your type of business. Research the trade press, or make enquiries with other similar companies that have been through the sale process.
- The lower the perceived risk, the higher The Multiplier.

An example

Here is an example to give you an idea of how the principle of The Multiplier works in practice. Let's say there are two very similar businesses on the market for sale, Business A and Business B:

1. **Business A** is a small construction and building business. It has been around for many years. Its future maintainable earnings were $200,000. The business can tap into what is projected to be a solid building boom. The business has mature systems and processes, including work management, finance and safety. It has three long-term skilled employees who are able to operate independently of the owner. They are also well known by customers and they want to stay after the sale.
2. **Business B** is a similar construction company operating in the same market, for

almost as long, with the same future maintainable earnings of $200,000. However, Business B relies heavily on the owner. He is 'old school', putting little down in the way of repeatable processes or documentation, relying on his experience and knowledge. He has three loyal staff but they operate only on his direction. These employees are not sure they will work for a new manager. Customers also deal almost exclusively with the owner.

I'm sure you can work out which one you'd prefer to buy.

The value of Business A is likely to be higher than Business B. This is because Business A is more likely to maintain the same profitability after the old owner has gone. Therefore, the multiplier you use to value Business A will be higher than Business B.

If the future maintainable earnings are $200,000 for both businesses, what might they be worth? What value do we multiply the $200,000 by to determine their value? You and I cannot determine this accurately from the information I have provided. We do not know what businesses like this have sold for in the recent past. We are not sure if there are any conventions used for businesses like this. It is rare to see multipliers greater than 3 in small businesses. Many are less than 1 because of the high failure rates (higher risks) associated with small businesses. To finalise our simple example, I have made an 'educated guess' at what their values might be.

Business A: I believe the multiplier would be around 2, making it worth around 2 x $200,000 = $400,000.

Business B: I believe the multiplier would be less than 1, making it worth less than $200,000.

As you can see there is a high level of estimation in this process. The experts operating in the market will be able to determine the value much better than our 'educated guess'.

☞ *Even more important than the expert's assessment of value is the value the buyer and seller agree upon. In the end, this is the only thing that will determine the real value of the business.*

Other valuation methods

1. Asset-based method

This method involves adjusting each asset and liability on the balance sheet to reflect the fair market value. This does not use the depreciated or book value of assets in the balance sheet. Once this has been done, the assets and liabilities are summed to give a net value. This is the most common way a business is valued when it is to be liquidated.

It could also be used if the value of the assets in the business is much greater than the value determined by the Historical Earnings Method. Basically, this means the business has a lot of reasonably high-valued assets but it is not generating a lot of profit from those assets.

This method does not consider the earnings of the business and is of little use if the business is being valued as a going concern. However, it is worth completing this calculation as well as doing the Historical Earnings Method, as it will indicate the lowest price the business should attract.

2. Market-based method

This method compares the price paid for similar businesses sold in the same area as the business being considered for sale. It is difficult to compare two businesses as they may look the same externally, but have been operated very differently.

Only those who have detailed insight into the sale price of those similar businesses will be able to assess this. Most business sales are done confidentially.

Like the asset-based method, the market-based method should also be considered in the valuation, not to replace the Historical Earnings Method, but to test its credibility.

Summary

Some final points of summary on valuing small businesses:

- Whether you want to buy or sell a small business, you should have some understanding of how to value one.
- The things that make a business more valuable for sale will also prove to make a business stronger and more manageable, even if you have no intention of selling. These are consistent profitability, good systems and processes, and a business that can operate independently of the owner.
- The best method to use, if valuing a business as a going concern, is the Historical Earnings Method. It considers the most critical aspect of a business: its likely future profitability.
- The more transferable the business and the more unencumbered with debts, the greater the value of the business will be.
- The riskier the business appears, the lower will be its value. The Multiplier is the value by which a business's value is adjusted to reflect its level of risk.
- Other methods such as the asset- and market-based methods can assist in backing the Historical Earnings Method, but are not recommended when a business is being valued as a going concern.

Questions

- What do you think your business is currently worth?
- If you chose to sell it at some time in the future, what would you like to sell it for?

Chapter 15
Help! Where Can You Turn?

During all our previous conversations, I've put forward the theme that as the owner of a small business you have no choice but to know a little about all the key aspects of your business. However, you will never be able to know everything about everything. From time to time (or maybe more often), you'll need to call on help.

Being a small business owner with no, or very few, people working for you does not mean you need to operate in isolation. It's not about going it alone. You are in the perfect position to choose the type of people that can most help you to achieve what you are working towards.

> *"Like the 'right to remain silent' is the right to ask a question and expect a reasonable answer. You then not only learn from what you observe but learn from others."*
> — **Cherokee**

Far too many small business owners battle on singlehandedly without support. Outside assistance has a strong and positive impact on any business. Even the most experienced well-known and successful business people surround themselves with expertise to guide them. We have discussed how you can gain greater insight into yourself and how you need to be honest in doing so. What are you good at? Where are you weaker? What do you love doing? What do you dislike?

Far too many small business owners believe they don't need help, so fail to seek out the right people. They may be embarrassed to admit they're struggling or simply ignorant of what they do not know.

If they recognise they need help, they may believe it's too expensive and out of their reach. Yet failing to realise the value of external input is costly and the impact of suffering in silence could be huge.

In the areas where you lack skills, *you need to find the best advice you can afford*. It is just as important to remember that good advice does not always come with a high price tag. Let's explore some places you can go for help.

Networking

The word 'networking' is commonly misinterpreted. Some people look upon it as wining and dining or rubbing shoulders with people who plug their businesses constantly (the kind we'd prefer to avoid). For small businesses, networking is one of the most powerful ways to share experiences, pursue referral work and build up a circle of like-minded business allies. It's very important that you purposefully build time into your calendar to network.

When networking, always ask yourself: Is this particular networking helping my business? This will save you precious time networking in less effective places. There may well be business people you enjoy meeting with for a coffee or a drink. Such social outings are great, but if it's not benefiting your business, it's just a drink, not networking. Enjoy it for what it is — time with friends.

You may feel awkward meeting with other people when their motives are solely to chase business. Some of us are also uncomfortable with overtly selling our own business, or even talking about it. Remember, the people you are networking with are there for the same reason as you and probably have the same challenges and interests.

Small business networking comes easier to some than others, but the good news is business networking skills can be learnt and improved. With time, you will become increasingly comfortable and see the significant benefits networking can bring.

Networking groups

There are many structured networking groups around the world. Some will be locally based, some are at a national level, and some are international. They may cover specific businesses or any small business that wants to attend.

An example of an international business networking group that I know increases business activity for the businesses involved is Business Network International (BNI). There are more than 150,000 members worldwide in this particular network.

If you look around your town or city, there are sure to be similar groups that meet for the sole purpose of improving their businesses.

Online networking

We discussed the power of being online to connect with your customers and increase sales. Social media offers a means for business owners like you to access a huge array of other small business people across the world. This allows you to interact with these people, put forward your own ideas and seek discussions on a huge range of topics.

Blogging has been a part of life on the web since the mid-1990s. What started as a personal form of interaction has grown substantially and has now become a credible means for mainstream business people to communicate.

Likewise, social media sites offer an extremely effective platform to connect with fellow business owners.

Social media sites, like Facebook and LinkedIn, allow you to join group discussions and post articles that you may want to discuss. In doing this, it will raise your credibility in the eyes of the reader, and may draw out people during the discussion that you can link up with directly.

There are also sites where you can read and post business articles online, including HubPages, EzineArticles and SlideShare.

The biggest issue for you to contend with is which media to use, how to maximise the benefit from it, and ultimately how it will add value to your business. If you have used a social media site for personal reasons, you probably have a good idea how much time you can spend on there. If you are using it for networking, like any other form, you should question the value it brings your business.

Advocacy groups

As a small business, you do not have the time or financial resources to have any real influence on political or other decision-makers. There are huge numbers of groups that exist to represent their small business members. There are as many advocacy organisations as there are types of businesses and industries.

These are a few examples of the more internationally recognised advocacy groups:

- Business New Zealand
- Chambers of Commerce (worldwide)
- Federation of Small Business (FSB) (UK)
- National Federation of Independent Businesses (USA)
- European Association of Craft, Small and Medium-Sized Enterprises (UEAPME) (European Union)
- Council of Small Business Australia (COSBA).

These groups can deliver a wide range of potential services, many for a fairly modest annual fee. These services may typically include:

- Lobbying on regulatory change

- Training
- Helpline and advice
- Networking groups
- Newsletters and notices
- Updates on changes to laws and regulations
- Discounts and special offers with suppliers.

Ongoing learning

You will find no problems getting your hands on an absolute wealth of material on how you could improve your small business. Your issue is filtering through the noise to find what you want.

If you have a question, the web will produce an answer (right or wrong). Amazon and other online booksellers cover a huge array of topics that are applicable to your small business. Many banks, advocacy groups and other organisations offer free or very low-cost education programmes for small business owners.

Remember to be selective and use your time most efficiently.

Who is advising you . . . and are they any good?

Now that you have established your skills and deficiencies, have a think about where you most need help and who currently advises you. Understand the drivers and motives of those advisors. Have you a list of the experts you may need from time to time or on an ongoing basis? Remember, you decide when to call for help and you make the decisions, not your advisors. Here are a few of the most common experts I see small businesses, including my own, turning to on a regular basis:

- Accountants
- Administration businesses
- Bank managers and the bank's business advisors
- Business mentors
- Lawyers
- Insurance brokers
- Recruitment companies
- Human resource experts
- Web developers
- Graphic designers
- Small business marketing experts
- Social media specialists
- Angel investors
- Non-bank debt funders
- Franchisors.

And there are likely to be more.

Many may apply to you at different stages in the life of your business. In some cases, these people may be trusted colleagues and they may give their advice at no cost. However, understand that the advisor you are meeting with may also be trying to make a living and you both need to be comfortable about where the line is between free advice and paid expertise.

These people may also be seeking to build a relationship with you to attract your business over the long term. If you see there is no connection with the person or no benefit to you from using them, don't be afraid to move on to other experts.

Summary

The key things to remember about this chapter are:

- There is nothing heroic about running your small business in isolation. No matter how experienced you are (or think you are), you will still need help.
- Find the very best help you can afford. Some great help can even be free.
- If your advisors are not helping you, you don't trust them or you feel they are not acting in your best interests, bid them farewell and find help that you can depend on. You deserve better.
- Take a look at my website for more information on how to make your small business the success you are seeking

www.under5smallbusiness.com

Questions

- Who are your most trusted business advisors?
- Where would you turn if you were struggling to cope in your business?

Chapter 16
Conclusion

So how can we pull this all together? We have covered a lot of territory and you may feel a little overwhelmed with everything that you need to do to achieve the success you seek in your small business.

☞ *Use the Strategic Plan Template at the back of the book to assist in summarising what you intend to do now. While I commend you for seeking a greater understanding of your business through a book like this, it is of little use if you don't act on this learning*

Lack of time is your biggest enemy

Before we close out our conversation, we need to talk about the most challenging aspect of bringing about change — *your time*.

People in all walks of life have the challenge of using the limited time they have in the best way they can. It comes down to the different priorities placed on the use of that time. As a small business owner it is no different for you. You can't create more time. You can only decide where your time is best spent to deliver the things that are most important to your business and also your life.

There is a very common, and often-used, piece of advice for business owners that you will hear. You need to work more **on the business** than **in the business**. I agree with this. I would make a slight variation though. You need to work on and in **all the different aspects** of the business that we've discussed. Some will take up most of your time. Others are just as critical but require less time.

When planning your calendar for the week, month or year, deliberately set aside an amount of time to cover the parts of the business that you are not devoting any time to at present.

Set aside an hour a week to review the past week and the week ahead. Then, on a monthly basis, reserve a couple of hours to review your accounts and business performance and to adjust activities for the next month. Allocate a few days in the year where you disappear and review where you are going, how you are going, and what changes you may need to make.

☞ *If you don't plan to change, you won't change.*

Now to conclude and summarise

You may have noticed that, throughout the book, I have posed many questions for you to consider. Where possible, I've asked open questions. These are questions that start with Who, What, Where, Why, When and How. These differ from closed questions that can be answered with a simple 'yes' or 'no'.

While I've provided advice to assist you, I've also posed these open questions to see if you are able to produce your own answers. You know your business, values, goals, strengths and weaknesses, and many other aspects of your business better than anyone. Sometimes just being asked the question will result in you challenging yourself and producing the answer. Rather than concluding with my thoughts or advice, I will pose a list of open questions to further explore your business and bring about ever-more realisations about your direction. I hope you ponder these and discover helpful answers for your business future.

How well did you go with the answers to these? While not every question will be relevant for every business owner, answer the ones that you think apply at this time in your business's life. The more you struggle to answer these, the more you may need to set aside some time to think and plan.

I truly hope our conversation has been of help to you. I would so love to hear how you achieve the success you seek. Your small business has the potential to bring you the lifestyle you want, greater happiness and meaning. As you no doubt know, these don't come easily. You have to be prepared to change if you're not achieving the level of happiness you desire and put in the effort required to reach what you consider success.

If you do, the rewards will come.

If you need more help on any topics in this book please visit our website where we have videos, questionnaires, templates and additional detail to help you further:

www.under5smallbusiness.com

Complete Your Strategic Plan

Business Name

Time Period Plan Covers

My Business's Core Purpose

My Core Values

Value 1	Value 2	Value 3	Value 4	Value 5

Associated Behaviours

My Business's 3 to 5 Year Goals

My Personal Wellbeing Rules

SWOT

My Business's Strengths

My Business's Weaknesses

External Threats

External Opportunities

Marketing

My point of Difference is:

My ideal customers are

My product or service meets these needs:

My pricing will be:

The traditional promotion I intend to use will be:

The online promotion I intend to use will be:

Staff

The plans for my staff will be:

My 12 Month Priorities

1.

2.

3.

4.

5.

Key Performance Indicators (KPIs) I will monitor

KPI	Target
Sales	
%Gross Profit	
Net Profit	

The Author's Story

In my work with many small business owners, one thing I'm always very conscious of when I discuss their business is that I'm entering a significant part of their lives. As the owner of a small business, your work, business and personal life are intimately intertwined. It's not always clear where one stops and one starts. Your business can reflect a great deal about you, what you're passionate about, what you're good at and where you're more limited. I'm always very humbled when a small business owner like you opens up their business to me seeking help. I never take this for granted.

While the book is about helping you, it's only reasonable that I share with you a little about my business, my world and my life. In the end, you were prepared to spend your time with me through this book. So it's the least I can do.

I am a baby boomer born in the early 1960s in a family of five kids. I discussed a little about my father and mother's business in early chapters of the book. So you'll know that I grew up with parents who ran a small business. Dad is now 84, but he recently wired my sister's four-bedroom home renovation. I guess some of us never retire.

I had a fierce competitive streak and ambition to achieve to a high standard from an early age. As a kid, I saw how hard Dad and Mum worked and had no intention of starting my own business. I sought an easier path.

I graduated as an engineer and was lucky enough to pursue my career for a few years around the world (in Asia, Europe and Africa). This was a great experience as a young single guy, doing engineering in large infrastructure projects worldwide.

Soon I met and married my wonderful wife, Judy. That was more than 20 years ago. A few years later, we had two beautiful kids, Laura and Michael. I completed an MBA in Finance. Then from the early 1990s, I started my journey through the ranks of management. I moved from frontline leadership roles to middle management and finally on to senior executive management. In my last position, I was accountable for about 400 people covering four large industrial sites. My division pulled in about $US 1 billion of revenue per year. I had budgets in excess of $US 100 million and traded energy into hedge and futures markets. I was able to study business at Columbia University in New York City and I was knocking on the door of a few CEO positions. I was making a very healthy salary, owned two houses, had a loving family (both immediate and more distant) and was pretty fit, running, paddling and cycling. My competitive and ambitious streak was telling me "Hey Bob, you've really made it!"

Little did I know that, while I considered myself to be very self-aware, things were very wrong. The work environment I was in was completely at odds with my core values. My stress levels were at an all-time extreme and worsening, even though I was telling myself, as a senior executive, I was in complete control. My family was seeing less and less of me and, when they did see me, I was preoccupied and distant. My work stopped giving me the meaning it once had, but I was too blinded by what I thought 'success' was to accept this. It was not surprising that eventually reality hit home, rather brutally.

I slid into a deep and very serious clinical depression. I could not return to work for more than three months. On returning to work, I realised it was an unsustainable situation. Eventually, after a very difficult eight months, I left my job to regroup and assess what success really was for me and where I should go next.

I went back to university and studied psychology (I saw myself as a bit of a science project). In the months after that, I started helping a number of small and mid-sized businesses with the skills I'd gained in 25 years of big business. I started recognising what really gave me meaning — helping others. My wife and I understood there was a significant need to help small businesses with affordable, low-cost advice, so we set up our small advisory business . . . not completely sure if we could make a living from it.

This was almost three years ago. Since then, I've offered support to a wide range of businesses. We are now working to ensure that we continue to meet our core purpose of helping people and other businesses while building a 'successful' small business of our own — one where success means something quite different now to what it did when I was flying up the corporate ladder.

This experience demonstrated to me that understanding your values, core purpose, building emotional resilience, and understanding what brings true meaning and happiness to you were not just areas to manage in our personal lives. They go to the heart of running, and enjoying, any business of any size.

Thank you for reading and all the best in your small business.

All the very best to you.

Bob Weir

Appendix — Resource Material

In writing this book, I have tapped into my experience and the experience of colleagues, and I've accessed a lot of books, websites, articles, scientific papers and blogs. It is appropriate that I should reference all the literature that has, in some way, influenced the content of this book. Also, if you are so inclined, you may wish to dig a little deeper in areas I have touched on in the book. Have fun!

General Books

Michael E. Gerber. *The E Myth Revisited — Why Most Small Businesses Don't Work and What to Do About It*. 1995.

Gerrish, Leader and Crocker. *Flying Solo*. 2011.

Andrew Griffiths. *The Big Book of Small Business*. 2011.

Laura Humphreys. *Liber8 Your Business*. 2013.

Nicholas Humphrey. *The Small Business Guide*. 2010.

Larry Keltto. *The Solopreneur Life — 42 Solo-Business Owners Speak the Truth on Dreaming Big, Failing Forward and Calling Your Own Shots*. 2011.

Stephen C. Lundin. *FISH*. 2000.

Wellbeing, Resilience and Optimism

Aldridge and Lavender. *The Impact of Learning on Health*. Education, Resources and Information Center (ERIC). 2000.

Dawson and Reid. 'Fatigue, Alcohol and Performance Impairment'. *Nature* magazine. 1997.

Sarah Edelman. *Change Your Thinking*. 2013.

Martin Seligman. *Learned Optimism — How to Change Your Mind and Your Life*. 2006.

Matthew P. Walker et al. *The Human Emotional Brain without Sleep*. 2007.

Website: World Health Organization. 'Stress at the Workplace'. http://www.who.int/occupational_health/topics/stressatwp/en/

Andrew Zolli and Ann Marie Healy. *Resilience: Why Things Bounce Back*. 2012.

Stress

Documentary: *Stress: Portrait of a Killer*. National Geographic. https://www.youtube.com/watch?v=eYG0ZuTv5rs&feature=kp, 2008.

Keller A et al. *Does the Perception that Stress Affects Health Matter? The Association with Health and Mortality*. University of Wisconsin-Madison. 2012.

Nick Petrie. *Wake Up! The Surprising Truth about What Drives Stress and How Leaders Build Resilience*. The Centre for Creative Leadership. August 2013.

Robert M. Sapolsky. *Why Zebras Don't Get Ulcers*. 2004.

Happiness

Ed Diener and Robert Biswas-Diener. *Happiness — Unlocking the Mysteries of Psychological Wealth*. 2008.

Russ Harris. *The Happiness Trap*. 2008.

R. Inglehart and H.D. Klingemann. *Genes, Culture, and Happiness*. 2000.

Sonja Lyubomirsky. *The How of Happiness — A New Approach to Getting the Life You Want*. 1986.

Website: 'The Pursuit of Happiness — Bringing the Science of Happiness to Life'. http://www.pursuit-of-happiness.org

Personality Profiling

Daniel Goleman. *Emotional Intelligence — Why It Can Matter More Than IQ*. 1995.

Jerome Kagan. *Galen's Prophecy: Temperament in Human Nature*. 1997.

David Keirsey. *Please Understand Me II*. 1998.

Roman Krznaric, *Fortune* magazine. 'Have we all been duped by the Myers-Briggs test?'. 15 May 2013.

Mary McGuiness. *You've Got Personality — An introduction to the Personality Types Described by Carl Jung and Isabel Myers*. 2004.

William Moulton Marston. *Emotions of Normal People*. 1928.

Isabel Briggs Myers. *Introduction to TYPE*. 1998.

David J. Pittenger. *Cautionary Comments Regarding the Myers-Briggs Type Indicator*. University of Tennessee. 2005.

Website: 'Personality Theories, Types and Tests'. http://www.businessballs.com/personalitystylesmodels.htm

Decision Making

The many pieces of work by Dan Ariely and Daniel Kahneman;

"Emotion and Decision Making" Jennifer S. Lerner (Harvard) et. Al.

Cognition

Malcolm Gladwell. *Outliers — The Story of Success*. 2008.

Sheena Iyengar. *The Art of Choosing*. 2010.

David Kirsh. *A Few Thoughts on Cognitive Overload*. 2000.

George Miller. *The Magical Number Seven, Plus or Minus Two: Some Limits on Our Capacity for Processing Information*. March 1956.

Daniel T. Willingham. *Cognition — The Thinking Animal*. 2007.

Strategy and Strategy Execution

William Duggan. *Strategic Intuition*. 2007.

Stephen Lynch. *Business Execution for Results — A Practical Guide for Leaders of Small to Mid-Sized Firms*. 2013.

Willie Pietersen. *Strategic Learning*. 2010.

Michael Porter. *Competitive Strategy: Techniques for Analyzing Industries and Competitors*. 1980.

Terri L. Sjodin. *Small Message, Big Impact. The Elevator Speech Effect*. 2012.

Goals — Start-ups

Guy Kawasaki. *The Art of the Start*. 2004.

Online article: 'The Average Entrepreneur — What Type of People Start Up Businesses in the UK?' http://startups.co.uk/the-average-entrepreneur/. 2013.

Eric Ries. *The Lean Startup: How Relentless Change Creates Radically Successful Businesses*. 2011.

Goals — Growth

Charlie Gilkey. *The Small Business Life Cycle*. 2014.

Steven S. Little. *The 7 Irrefutable Rules of Small Business Growth*. 2005.

Goals — Succession

Aronoff, McClure and Ward. *Family Business Succession*. 2011.

Meir Liraz. *Business Succession Planning Checklist — A Step by Step Guide*. 2013.

Goals — Buying and Selling a Business

Rick Bisio. *The Educated Franchise — The How-To Book for Choosing a Winning Franchise*. 2011.

Ethan Crowther. *Buying a Small Business*. 2013.

Stieglitz and Sorkin. *Expensive Mistakes When Buying and Selling Companies*. 2010.

Fred S. Steingold. *The Complete Guide to Buying a Business*. 2011.

Goals — Business Succession

Craig E, Aronoff et al. *Family Business Succession — The Final Test of Greatness*.

Meir Liraz. *Business Succession Planning Checklist — A Step by Step Guide*. 2013.

Intellectual Property

Gary Jennings. *How to Register a Trademark*. 2013.

Richard Stim. *Patent, Copyright and Trademark: An Intellectual Property Desk Reference*. 2014.

Mathew Ward. *A Straightforward Guide to Intellectual Property and the Law*. 2011.

Marketing — General

Wayne Attwell. *Smart Marketing — Build a Powerful Brand through Need Satisfaction Marketing*. 2013.

Paul Christ. *Know This: Marketing Basics*. 2012.

Seth Godin. *Permission Marketing*. 1999.

Edmund Jerome. *McCarthy Basic Marketing — A Managerial Approach*. 1960.

Martin Lindstrom. *Buyology — How Everything We Believe About Why We Buy is Wrong*. 2008.

Jeanna Pool. *Marketing for Solos — The Ultimate How To Guide for Marketing Your One Person Small Business Successfully*. 2011.

Jack Trout. *Positioning: The Battle for Your Mind*. 2001.

Marketing — Brand

David A. Aaker. *Building Strong Brands*. 1996.

Scott Bedbury. *A New Brand World — 8 Principles for Achieving Brand Leadership in the 21st Century*. 2003.

Chris Malone and Susan T. Fiske. *The Human Brand: How We Relate to People, Products, and Companies*. 2013.

Marketing — Online

Mike Fishbein. *Growth Hacking with Content Marketing — How to Increase Website Traffic*. 2014.

Scott Fox. *Click Millionaires*. 2012.

Jason Holder. *How to Use Pinterest for Business*. 2013.

Marketing — Giving

Adam Braun. *The Promise of a Pencil — How an Ordinary Person Can Create Extraordinary Change*. 2014.

Elizabeth Dunn and Michael Norton. *Happy Money: The Science of Smarter Spending*. 2013.

Susan A. Hyatt. *Strategy for Good: Business Giving Strategies for the 21st Century*. 2010.

Blake Mycoskie. *Start Something that Matters*. 2012.

Systems, Processes and Day-to-Day

Bill Carreira. *Lean Manufacturing that Works*. 2005.

Daniel Markovitz. *A Factory of One*. 2011.

Ash Maurya. *Running Lean — Iterate from Plan A to a Plan that Works*. 2012.

Jason Tisbury. *Your 60 Minute Lean Business — 5S Implementation Guide*. 2012.

Accounting and Finances

Ethan Crowther. *Financial Ratios for Small Business*. 2013

Lita Epstein. *A Business Owner's Guide to Reading and Understanding Financial Statements*. 2012.

Lita Epstein. *Bookkeeping Workbook for Dummies*, 2007.

Bob Foster. Your How To Guide to Small Business Financial Statements. 2012.

Harvard Business Review — Guide to Finance Basics for Managers. 2014.

Thomas R. Ittelson. *Financial Statements — A Step-by-Step Guide to Understanding and Creating Financial Reports*. 2009.

Darrell Mullis and Judith Orloff. *The Accounting Game — Basic Accounting Fresh from the Lemonade Stand*. 2008.

Jim Porter. *How to Benchmark Your Business*. 2011.

Gene Siciliano. *Finance for Non-Financial Managers*. 2003.

John A. Tracey. *Accounting for Dummies*. 2013.

Funding Your Business

Mark Blayney. *Raising Finance for Your Business — A Nuts and Bolts Guide for SME Owners and Managers*. 2006.

Business Valuation

Kenneth A. Bonnici. *Value Your Business Now — A Down-to-Earth Step-by-Step Guide to Business Valuation*. 2012.

Lawrence W. Tuller. *The Small Business Valuation Book*. 2008.

Statistics, Research and Articles

Statistics New Zealand — General.

Australian Bureau of Statistics — General.

United States Census Bureau — General.

World Health Organization. http://www.who.int/occupational_health/topics/stressatwp/en/

World Health Organization. 'Gender and women's mental health'. http://www.who.int/mental_health/prevention/genderwomen/en/

'Sovereign Wellbeing Index — New Zealand's First Measure of Wellbeing'. Human Potential Centre and AUT University. 2013.

SAS Institute Inc. 'Measuring Strategy vs. Execution'. White Paper. 2013.

General Statistics on Big Business, mark-ups, advertising, crowdfunding:

http://www.incomediary.com/top-earning-companies-in-the-world

http://www.fastcompany.com/3021598/fast-feed/how-much-revenue-do-top-companies-make-each-second

http://finance.yahoo.com/news/20-products-giant-markups-115730856.html

file://localhost/(http/::www.statista.com:statistics:286333:most-advertised-brands-in-the-us:)

http://www.statista.com/chart/1492/ad-spend-per-capita/

http://www.statista.com/statistics/251572/development-in-worldwide-crowdfunding-funding-volume/

http://www.forbes.com/sites/elainepofeldt/2013/06/29/the-rise-of-the-million-dollar-one-person-business/

Index

Sapolsky, Robert, 17, 18
scenario planning, 88, 89
search engine optimisation (SEO), 112–114
self-knowledge, 31
Seligman, Martin, 19
Serenity Prayer, 12
Shareholder's equity, 162
Slideshare, 119
Stockdale, James (Admiral), 44
Subway (franchise), 77
succession, 40
Sun Tzu, 39

www.ingramcontent.com/pod-product-compliance
Lightning Source LLC
Chambersburg PA
CBHW050106220326
41598CB00043B/7395